T0316775

## COMMUNITY CAPITALISM IN CHINA

This book proposes to end the dichotomous view of the state and the market, and capitalism and communism, by examining the local institutional innovation in three villages in China and presents *community capitalism* as an alternative to the neoliberal model of development. Community is both the unit of redistribution and the entity that mobilizes resources to compete in the market; collectivism creates the boundary that sets the community apart from the outside and justifies and sustains the model. Community capitalism differs from Mao-era collectivism, when individual interests were buried in the name of collective interests and market competition was not a concern. It also deviates from cooperatives such as Israeli kibbutzim, in that there are obvious hierarchies in the community and people pursue the accumulation of wealth and modern conveniences. Nonetheless, this book demonstrates the embeddedness of the market in community, showing how social relations, group solidarity, power, honor, and other values play an important role in these villages' social and economic organization.

Xiaoshuo Hou is an assistant professor of sociology at St. Lawrence University. Her research interests include the sociology of development, economic sociology, sociology of organizations, and the socioeconomic transformations in China. She has published extensively in *The Journal of Asian Studies, Theory and Society, Contemporary Sociology, Ethnic and Racial Studies*, and *Theory, Culture & Society*. Currently, she is coediting the five-volume *Wiley-Blackwell Encyclopedia of Race, Ethnicity, and Nationalism*. She received her PhD in sociology from Boston University.

# Community Capitalism in China

## The State, the Market, and Collectivism

### XIAOSHUO HOU
St. Lawrence University

# CAMBRIDGE
## UNIVERSITY PRESS

32 Avenue of the Americas, New York NY 10013-2473, USA

Cambridge University Press is part of the University of Cambridge.

It furthers the University's mission by disseminating knowledge in the pursuit of education, learning and research at the highest international levels of excellence.

www.cambridge.org
Information on this title: www.cambridge.org/9781107448780

First published 2013
First paperback edition 2014

*A catalogue record for this publication is available from the British Library*

*Library of Congress Cataloguing in Publication data*
Hou, Xiaoshuo, 1982–
Community capitalism in China : the state, the market, and collectivism / Xiaoshuo Hou.
p. cm.
Includes bibliographical references and index.
ISBN 978-1-107-03046-6 (hbk.)
1. Capitalism – China. 2. Communism – China. 3. Rural development – China. 4. China – Economic conditions – 2000–
5. China – Economic policy – 2000– I. Title.
HC427.95.H685 2013
330.12′20951–dc23 2012033217

ISBN 978-1-107-03046-6 Hardback
ISBN 978-1-107-44878-0 Paperback

*To Huiqin, Ling, and Tao*

# Contents

# Preface

C. Wright Mills, in his book *The Sociological Imagination*, writes that "neither the life of an individual nor the history of a society can be understood without understanding both" (1959: 3). My parents' generation is often called the "lost generation," as they were caught between the Mao years and the reforms. When they were young, energetic, and idealistic, they were placed in one political campaign after another and sent down to the countryside for reeducation. When they were finally to become the backbone of China, the reforms opened up new opportunities for those younger than them and everything they were good at was all of a sudden no longer treasured: the "iron rice bowl" turned into layoffs, ration coupons were replaced by cash, political loyalty became secondary to technical expertise. Their lives were full of surprises. My generation was born after the reforms and deemed to be luckier than any of the previous generations. However, as China's reforms go deeper, marketization and privatization have further undermined the social welfare benefits once enjoyed by my parents' generation, and surging living costs and more visible inequalities have again posed unprecedented challenges to my generation. If anything, to own an apartment and get married seems to be a far-fetched dream for some. Our personal biographies are indeed connected with the larger social context, and that cannot be truer for the millions of Chinese that have been thrown into the tides of social change where learning to swim with the currents is the only option. This book is exactly about how people at the most grassroots level in China cope with social change in search of both economic prosperity and social solidarity.

Since the Industrial Revolution, urbanization and industrialization have been prescribed as the vehicles of development, and they are, not surprisingly, also touted as the goals of the Chinese reform. Nonetheless, for the rural residents, urbanization and industrialization have been anything but romantic as they struggle to find their new identities and positions in society. Some of them migrate to the cities to explore a new life yet often find themselves lost in the "black hole" of dreams; others stay or are forced behind, looking for a way of living beyond self-subsistence farming. Therefore, this is also a book about those in rural China who are experiencing the dual transformation from an agrarian society to a more industrialized society and from a planned economy to a more market-oriented economy. Of course, the protagonists of the stories are neither successful peasants-turned-private-entrepreneurs nor migrant workers nor street vendors; they are members of industrialized villages with collectively owned enterprises. They pool resources together – sometimes land and other times even labor, cash, and social networks – to support those enterprises, and at the same time receive dividends as shareholders. As a result, the collectively owned enterprises give the villagers a base for competing in the market and simultaneously provide them with a safety net that has gradually been eroded by the market and evaded by the state.

Furthermore, this book is an exploration of local institutional innovations that end the dichotomous view of the state and the market, communism and capitalism, and offers the perspective of "both/and" rather than "either/or." Such an alternative path of development to the neoliberal model is captured in what I call community capitalism, where community is both an entity of resource mobilization and a basis for redistribution. It is different from the old collectivism in the Mao era when individual interests were buried in the name of collective interests and market competition was not a concern. It also deviates from cooperatives like kibbutzim in Israel in that there are obvious hierarchies in those communities and people do pursue the accumulation of wealth and all the modern conveniences. Nonetheless, it departs from the prototypical market economy assumed by neoclassical economics, as social relations, group solidarity, power, honor, and values play an important role in its social and economic organization.

Book writing is no doubt a collective project, although the author oftentimes takes the sole credit, so here I would like to extend my gratitude for the generous help and support from various institutions and individuals who made this book possible.

My first and foremost thanks go to the kindness of my interviewees in the three villages described in this book – Nanjie, Huaxi, and Shangyuan. Without their courage and wisdom, these local institutional innovations would not have been possible; without their frankness and trust, I could not have completed my research and documented their experiences. The same gratitude goes to my friends and contacts that facilitated my initial entry into those villages and provided me with their hospitality during my field trips to China.

Teachers and mentors at Boston University provided the intellectual roots for this book. I owe a tremendous debt to my doctoral advisor, John Stone. Without his support, encouragement, care, and humor, I could not have survived my PhD years or written this book. His kindness and friendship made the transition to a new culture a lot easier for an international student. He carefully read every chapter of the original dissertation as well as the various versions of the book manuscript and always offered thoughtful comments. His unreserved confidence in me motivated me to get the book published. I could not be any luckier to have him as my mentor. My other dissertation readers, Joe Fewsmith, Dan Monti, Rob Weller, and Julian Go, all supplied critical insights and invaluable advice to both my academic pursuits and my life. Joe Fewsmith inspired me to expand the scope of my research to include Huaxi and Shangyuan, and has always been generous with his time, care, and support. Dan Monti involved me in various projects and shared his wisdom and attitudes toward life. Rob Weller introduced me to the world of anthropology and a bottom-up approach of studying China. Julian Go, Alya Guseva, Polly Rizova, and Emily Barman have always been my role models as young and accomplished scholars and offered me their help and friendship.

Boston University's Graduate Research Abroad Fellowship funded the field trips for my dissertation, and St. Lawrence University's Freeman Grant partially supported my latest travel to the sites in 2010. I am indebted to them for their financial support.

Earlier versions of some of the chapters have been published elsewhere or presented at conferences and seminars. Portions of Chapter 1 and Chapter 5 appear in "From Mao to the Market: Community Capitalism in Rural China," *Theory, Culture & Society* 28 (2): 48–68. I am grateful to the anonymous reviewers who offered insightful comments. I have also benefited from input from audiences at annual meetings of the American Sociological Association and Eastern Sociological Society and at other venues. I would like to especially thank Moshe Banai, who generously offered his research on Israeli kibbutzim as comparisons for my cases and believed in the value of my research. Don Tomaskovic-Devey also generously shared his thoughts and suggestions.

In the course of revising the manuscript for publication, I have received thoughtful comments from the anonymous reviewers who helped strengthen the conceptualization in the book. Pat Rieker and Tian Yu Cao shared their insight and experience in book publishing and offered sound advice. My colleagues at St. Lawrence University have always been support-ive; they motivated me to become a more disciplined writer in the midst of teaching. At Cambridge University Press, I could not ask for a more patient, supportive, and experienced editor than Scott Parris. Without him, this book would probably be a manuscript forever. Kristin Purdy was extremely responsive, professional, and friendly, which greatly helped reduce a writ-er's anxiety before the production of the book. I also owe tremendously to my copyeditor, Susan Kauffman of PETT Fox, Inc., and the production team at Newgen, who made every effort to ensure the quality of the book.

Family is an important social institution in China, and a person's identity is often defined by their family relations. Therefore, last but not least, I am thankful to my family. Born in an intellectual family, I knew that Marx and Engels both had large beards when I was three. Having two philosopher parents, I have been engaged in family debates since childhood. My parents, Xiao Ling and Hou Huiqin, are my best friends and finest mentors. I have learned from them how to be a kind human being and a scholar with pas-sion and integrity. To them I owe life, education, opportunities, love, friend-ship, and guidance. My husband, Tao, has always been my biggest supporter and cheerleader, though the prolonged process of researching and writing often meant being away from him. I thank him for the constructive critique he offered as an economist, for his deepest confidence in me – more than what I have in myself – and for his priceless love and emotional support. My grandparents, uncles, aunts, cousins, and in-laws have all been an insepa-rable part of my life and provided their support in a multitude of ways. I dedicate this book to my family.

ONE

# The Curse Revisited

## The Dynamics of Social Change in China

Planning and market forces are not the essential difference between socialism and capitalism. A planned economy is not the definition of socialism, because there is planning under capitalism; the market economy happens under socialism, too. Planning and market forces are both ways of controlling economic activity. The essence of socialism is liberation and development of the productive forces, elimination of exploitation and polarization, and the ultimate achievement of prosperity for all.... In short, if we want socialism to achieve superiority over capitalism, we should not hesitate to draw on the achievements of all cultures and to learn from other countries including the developed capitalist countries, all advanced methods of operation and techniques of management that reflect the laws governing modern socialized production.

Deng Xiaoping (1992)

After a remarkable three-decade period of double-digit economic growth, China has surpassed Japan to become the second-largest economy in the world, only surpassed by the United States. With its increasing economic power and political clout, China now frequently appears in Western newspapers, magazines, talk shows, academic journals and meetings, and even in the 2010 midterm political campaign advertisements in the United States, as everybody is eager to assess this awakening dragon and at the same time predict its future.

Life is confusing during times of radical social change: critics and eulogists coexist, and there are often mixed feelings of hope and despair. Like eighteenth-century England and France, China is at an equally critical juncture. Some predict that China could replace the United States in a few decades to become the next superpower; others foresee a fate similar to that of Japan three decades ago: eventually bubbles would burst and China would be trapped in stagnation, if not degenerate into a total calamity. From a Western point of view, it may be difficult to make sense of the many

1

paradoxes involved in China's development. The old modernization theory that attributes Western ascendency to market capitalism, a scientific revolution, a consumer society, the Protestant work ethic, and political participation and representation, and thus suggests that developing countries should emulate the same institutions to rise in the modern world, does not seem to serve China well.

However, even a casual observer can see the rising skyscrapers, sprawling construction sites, bustling shopping malls and entertainment centers, nouveaux riches who indulge themselves in all kinds of status symbols from Lamborghinis to Hermès handbags,[1] and even the not-so-rich who are striving for a "petty bourgeoisie" (*xiaozi*) lifestyle by actively acquiring the same items that comprise the dream of the American middle class: a car, a house, a well-paid white-collar job, and diverse leisure activities. For many, socialism with Chinese characteristics is indeed capitalism, not only in terms of economic institutions but also the increasingly capitalistic values among many Chinese today who work long hours and give their first priority to moneymaking activities and the accumulation of wealth above anything else. Yet one does not have to be a China specialist to notice the differences between China and the advanced capitalist countries. The question is then whether these differences indicate a transitory stage or an alternative path. Has the old Weberian curse that the Chinese do not have a work ethic of this-worldly asceticism and the purposive-legal rationality, both essential to the development of capitalism, been reversed?

In the following section, I first review some of the paradoxes evident in the process of China's reform and how current scholarship evaluates them, then present my interpretation, and finally analyze how this book can enrich the debate.

### "Partial Reform"

The metamorphosis of Chinese society seems to be full of ambiguities that prohibit any easy labeling; one probably needs to look beyond the dichotomous views of capitalism and communism, state and market, in order to make sense of it. The first noticeable paradox is that China manages to run on two unbalanced legs that are often seen as incompatible: a Communist Party-led state and an increasingly liberalized economy. Of course, contrary

---

[1]  China is now the second-largest market for luxury goods, accounting for 27.5% ($9.6 billion) of the global market in 2009. See Donny Kwok's report at http://www.reuters.com/article/idUSTOE67107820100806.

to neoliberalists, who believe that the only problem facing transitional economies is insufficient marketization, new institutionalists have long realized that an effective state is often an integral part of successful economic development and calls for "bringing the state back in" (Evans et al. 1985). New institutional economists such as Douglass North (1981) also propose that the state is an important actor in defining property rights and providing institutionalized norms to reduce transaction costs and thus recognize the importance of social institutions that underlie economic activities, although such propositions are still within the framework of market efficiency and instrumental rationality.

Those who study dependent development in Latin America and the East Asian developmental state further regard state capacity and state autonomy as key factors in analyzing socioeconomic transitions (White 1988; Evans 1989; Woo-Cumings 1999). However, whether deeper state intervention will bring about more state autonomy and a better capacity for coherent corporate action, will lead to the erosion and division of the state from civil society, or will cause rampant rent-seeking activities from those in power, is "complexly contingent, explicable only by the basis of careful comparative-historical research" (Rueschemeyer and Evans 1985:70). Nonetheless, the kind of "market fundamentalism" (Stiglitz 2002) displayed in the neoliberal version of development exaggerates the magic power of the market yet overlooks the complex relations between the state, the market, and social relations.

In contrast with other former socialist countries, China took what is called "a gradualist approach" to reform as opposed to the "shock therapy" adopted by Russia and Eastern Europe (Walder 1996). This reform strategy can be understood from three aspects.

First, unlike other former socialist countries, despite the relative economic liberalization, liberal democracy has not yet taken root in China, and much of the Soviet-Leninist mechanism remains untouched. China is still under the control of the Chinese Communist Party (CCP), and such a political fact is not likely to change in the near future. Therefore, the state/party combination will be the one to make and execute policies, constraining and controlling certain areas of development, societal change, and personal choices while rewarding others. Although direct elections have been formally implemented at the village level nationwide since the late 1990s, whether they will be scaled up to higher levels of administration remains to be seen. In the meantime, the CCP is searching for alternative ways to define and achieve democracy. This is clearly an attempt to legitimize the Chinese form of governance and counterbalance Western democratic ideals marked by a multiparty voting system and based on the Enlightenment values of liberty, equality, and fraternity. Evidence for this can be seen in the so-called intraparty democracy initiatives and the recent debate among Chinese scholars and politicians on whether there are any universal values.[2]

Second, in the economic realm, some sectors are more radically transformed than others. China's reform started with agriculture as opposed to the state-owned enterprises. The establishment of the "household responsibility system" (*jiating lianchan chengbao zerenzhi*)[3] in the late 1970s as a replacement of brigades and communes led to the sudden de-collectivization in rural China and the rapid marketization of farming and rural industries. However, the state's control over the production and pricing of grain and cotton was not relaxed until after more than two decades into the reform.[4] In urban areas, reform was much more incremental. State-owned enterprises (SOEs) had not been substantially altered until the late 1990s. Many industries, such as banking and telecommunications, remained in state control long after the reform began, and it was only following China's entry into the WTO in 2001 that some were put on the agenda to be subject to market mechanisms and open for global competition. While protecting and subsidizing the SOEs, China also encouraged the development of the non-state sector, especially collective enterprises and joint ventures. It is through this dual-track and piecemeal approach, as opposed to hollowing out public ownership overnight, that China has conducted its structural and ownership reforms.

Third, the more radical reform strategies are often first experimented on a small scale before they are spread nationwide. The aforementioned

---

[2]    See, for example, "The Debate over 'Universal Values' in China," by Jianmin Qi, *Journal of Contemporary China*, 2011, 20(72): 881–890. The debate was essentially over the question of whether the Western Enlightenment values are common pursuits for every human being despite economic, social, and cultural differences.

[3]    The household responsibility system grants peasants the use-right of land and the residual claimant right after turning over to the state a fixed proportion of what they have produced. The system does not involve the privatization of land, but restores the way of organizing production to that before the collectivization in Maoist China – that is, the family as the basic unit for farming and production.

[4]    For a discussion of the development of agricultural commerce in China and the fluctuation of state policies in grain and cotton production, see Terry Sicular, "Redefining State, Plan and Market: China's Reforms in Agricultural Commerce," in Andrew G. Walder (ed.), *China's Transitional Economy* (Oxford, UK: Oxford University Press, 1996), pp. 58–84. In 2004, the state passed a new grain-trading regulation to further reform the grain distribution system and to liberalize grain pricing and grain trading in accordance with market supply and demand. Economic units with different ownership forms were all allowed to compete in the grain market after passing the qualifying inspection. See *China Daily* (June 4, 2004).

household responsibility system, for example, was first created in the late 1970s by a group of commune members in Xiaogang Village located in Anhui province, and was then gradually adopted by other places in the early 1980s. Among the cities, Shenzhen, Zhuhai, Shantou, and Xiamen were the first four "special economic zones" opened to foreign investment and the global market in 1980 as a testing ground for economic reforms, joined in 1984 by fourteen more coastal cities with eleven "economic and technological development zones." Those economic zones received favorable state treatment including tax reductions and exemptions. In 1988, China established the Hainan special economic zone, and Shanghai's Pudong was not open to foreign investment until 1990. From coastal cities to cities along the borders and rivers and finally to the hinterland, China has been opened to the world economy step by step.

China's "partial reform" has resulted in different evaluations. Scholars influenced by the modernization thesis and the critics of earlier partial reform in East European countries such as Hungary argue that China's gradualist approach is pathological and raises serious structural problems. For them, the market and a socialist state are incompatible, as government has nonfinancial interests in firms and firms can rely on government for subsidies and bailouts, leading to an underperforming economy. This is somewhat ironic if one looks at similar situations in advanced capitalist countries following the 2008 financial recession. Such a view was more prevalent in the 1980s and early 1990s (Wong 1986; Kornai 1992), but has never completely disappeared and has turned into disbelief about the sustainability of China's economic development and the prediction of its upcoming collapse (e.g., Chang 2001). A related assessment is that China has been relatively successful in the more radically reformed areas such as rural industries and other non-state sectors but less exceptional where reform has been incremental (Woo 1994; Huang 2008). Some argue that China's miraculous economic growth is a result of the transformation of an agrarian society, or largely rural society, into an industrial society, and is thus fundamentally different from the experience of a highly urbanized Soviet Union (Sachs and Woo 1994; Woo 1994). A more positive conclusion is that although China has its own problems, it is on the way to social change and economic improvement, and it thus acknowledges the accumulative effects of the reforms (Naughton 1994; Rawski 1994).

In recent years, from Joshua Cooper Ramo's *Beijing Consensus* (2004) to Giovanni Arrighi's *Adam Smith in Beijing* (2007) to the discussion of the possibility of a China model (*zhongguo moshi*) since the global recession, China's developmental strategy has been seen by some as a challenge to the

Western triumphalism as it has seemingly defied the doctrines of neoliberalism and can possibly provide developing countries with an alternative path of development that counters the teachings of privatization, marketization, and liberalization advocated by the Washington Consensus. In other words, Fukuyama (1992) was far too early to announce "the end of history," as the fight over the ultimate goal of development and the proper social, economic, and political institutions leading to that outcome continues. Others, however, see China's economic success as the victory of neoliberalism that is largely based on the exploitation of the vast pool of cheap labor by foreign investment and an increasingly open economy that releases domestic entrepreneurship. Any problems, it is claimed, are the consequences of deviating from the Washington Consensus (Huang 2008; Yao 2011). The question of whether there is indeed a "China model," or any components of such a model, is beyond the scope of this book,[5] but I hope to offer a new perspective on China's development by analyzing the relationship between the state, the market, and social relations. I call it *community capitalism* and discuss the concept further later in the chapter.

## The Market Transition Debate

Related to the "partial reform" issue are the questions of who benefits financially and who gains power as market mechanisms are introduced, and what accounts for the vitality of a private economy in post-socialist China. There are three main bodies of literature analyzing these issues.

The first is the market transition theory initiated by Victor Nee in 1989 in a study of household income in rural China (Nee 1989, 1991, 1992, 1996; Nee and Cao 1999; Cao and Nee 2000). It is based on Karl Polanyi's typology of modes of economic integration (1957): reciprocity, redistribution, and market exchange.[6] Institutional change in post-socialist

---

[5]    I discussed this topic in a conference paper entitled "All Roads Lead to Washington?: Controversies over the China Model," which was presented on May 29, 2011, at "Visions and Perspectives: Global Studies in the 21st Century" held in Nanjing, China.

[6]    According to Polanyi, the market is not something natural but is situated in social institutions. In addition, the economy cannot be seen as equal to the market, as there have been other forms of economic organization through human history, such as reciprocity and redistribution. Reciprocity is based on symmetric groups exchanging favors, whereas redistribution is where goods flow in and out of a center or central authority that determines entitlements. In both cases, economic activities define and are also defined by social relationships and social standing. Reciprocity, redistribution, and market exchange are not different stages of development but can coexist. Here Polanyi's original argument is actually different from the assumption made by the market transition theory that views the market as the end result.

societies is conceptualized as a transition from a redistributive econ-omy to a market economy. This account mainly focuses on the chang-ing power – control over economic resources – in the transition of state socialism from state redistributors or government cadres to direct pro-ducers or private entrepreneurs. It emphasizes that the emerging markets open up opportunities for private businesses. As a result, the stratification system in socialist China will start to converge with capitalist societies, as market forces replace bureaucratic-redistributive mechanisms and the cadre elite with political capital loses its advantage to the business elite with human capital.

There are several variations on the market transition theory. One appar-ent contradiction to the market power thesis is the lingering redistribu-tive power and the persistence of socialist institutions (Bian and Logan 1996; Parish and Michelson 1996). Scholars who take a more state-centered approach argue that the shift from redistribution to market is simply a more effective way of government control, and the primary beneficiary of marketization is the same old "cadre elite," because the bureaucrats know well how to convert political power into economic capital (Rona-Tas 1994). Although market mechanisms have created more incentives than political directives, and people who have more technical skills can also gain upward mobility, political credentials remain an important determinant of elite position, thus generating "a divided elite" (Walder 1995).

Another modification of the market transition theory is related to its dichotomy of market and redistribution. Walder (1996), for example, argues that market allocation per se has no implications for the distribution of power and income. Those two ideal types need to be seen in a specific context, as the pace of change and arrangements of institutional mixes may vary. Scholars since then have started to pay more attention to the process of transition rather than the outcome (Zhou 2000; Walder 2002, 2003).

An important limitation of the market transition theory, as Nan Lin (1995) correctly points out, is its view of a market economy as the end product, and anything other than a market economy should not be seen as transitory and may well persist or even provide possibilities for alterna-tives. In addition, the market itself is embedded in different social relations, institutional setups, and sense-making mechanisms; therefore, the market in reality is not a uniform abstract structure as in the ideal-type model of neoclassical economics. In other words, the free, self-regulating market is nothing but a myth. Furthermore, it does not account for local variations under the same set of state reform policies (Lin 1995). How local govern-ments and people interpret the market transition may well affect the path of development, and economic forces are intertwined with other processes of societal, ideological, cultural, and political change.

The second body of literature is based on market-bureaucracy interaction (Bruun 1993, 1995; Wank 1995, 1996, 1999; Pearson 1997; Walder and Oi 1999), which suggests that China's private economy was born out of the interdependent, clientelist ties between local state officials and private entrepreneurs. As the state becomes more decentralized, greater autonomy and authority – and thereby more responsibilities – are passed down to local governments. Local state officials capitalize on their power and rely on private entrepreneurs for developing local economies, while private entrepreneurs depend on their ties with the local officials for resources and opportunities to initiate and develop their businesses. Therefore, there are complex relations between local governments and the central government, between local interests and national interests, and between different local governments.[7] Jean Oi, when analyzing rural China, characterizes the situation as "local state corporatism" seen as a variation of "state corporatism" in explaining the role of local governments. On the one hand, she uses the principal-agent model to explain the relation between the central state and local governments, in which the latter acts on behalf of the former. On the other hand, local governments "restrain the private sector from becoming an independent economic class" (Oi 1999:13) while often playing an entrepreneurial role in running the various firms within their territory.

Such a perspective provides new insight into China's transition, especially in the rural areas, as decentralization may not lead to the demise of central command and the dominance of the market. However, the patron-client or principal-agent ties first assume that political actors are rational, a transposition of the neoclassical economic model to the political field, and secondly they are based on dyadic ties. To what extent are local cadres rational? How do multiple ties affect one another? Clearly, cadres have other social responsibilities to meet, which is especially true for those in rural China. A village is not only a governing entity, but also a community and – for some industrialized villages – a large corporation, too. This approach fails to explain how cadres juggle their different social roles.

---

[7]    China has five levels of administration: the central government, provinces (including four municipalities directly under the central government, i.e., Beijing, Shanghai, Tianjin, Chongqing), cities/city-level counties, counties/city districts, and towns. Village governments are not counted as an official administrative level, but they are responsible for implementing the policies from the administrative levels above and are in direct contact with peasants.

The third analysis focuses on the sociocultural roots of transition (Hamilton and Kao 1990; Lin 1995; Whyte 1995, 1996; Lin and Chen 1999). It attributes the rising private economy to family-based or kinship-based obligation and trust. Market and command forces pull their strings through social networks. Family or kinship, as a traditional and enduring social institution, even after several decades of transformation under Mao, assumes two features: the declining power of the older generation and the survival of family solidarity. As a result, when economic reforms provide ideological and institutional support for private entrepreneurship, family becomes the dominant way of organizing economic undertakings, and family and pseudo-family networks become the major channels of resource mobilization. This approach complements the overemphasis on privatization or economic organization in the first two paradigms. However, just as it criticizes the market transition theory for not being able to cover local variations, it also fails to account for why one type of social network, such as kinship ties, is stronger in certain regions than in others, and why people choose one kind of ties over others.

These approaches provide three analytical tools to interpret China's transition: the first focuses on economic capital replacing political capital, and consequently market relations displacing political ties; the second looks at the clientelist ties between local cadres and private entrepreneurs and the role of the state, especially local state, in steering reforms; the third proposes the importance of family and pseudo-family networks in the development of a private economy. All three institutions – market, state/local state, and family and social networks – exert their influence on the Chinese economy, and depending on the social, economic, and political resources accessible to local communities, one form of economic organization may play a dominant role in different parts of China. If there is indeed a "China model," it certainly is not just one monolithic entity, but is composed of different local variations. For example, there is the more state-centered *Sunan Moshi* (Southern Jiangsu Model), but also the more entrepreneurial experience of Wenzhou and Shenzhen. Even in Wenzhou, in addition to the booming family businesses, there are still places where collective enterprises thrive, for instance in Shangyuan Village, one of the three cases in this book. So let a thousand flowers blossom but also let the flowers cross-pollinate – such is an exploratory and mutual learning process. The central state, meanwhile, plays the role of controller of last resort determining the road map of development and setting guidelines. The existence of local variations indicates that one needs to look at the macro-micro interaction to understand the dynamics of social change in China.

## Social Networks and the Market

Social networks, or *guanxi* in Chinese, define reciprocal obligation and mutual indebtedness. Many foreigners first get the idea of how *guanxi* works in China through the norm of gift giving. To put it simply, *guanxi* involves various personal ties: kinship ties, the "tong-ties" (including connections established through common place of origin, surname, school, work unit, army branch, etc.), the fictive kinship ties (e.g., sworn brotherhood/sisterhood/parenthood), and ties as members of the CCP or other parties and associations. In a word, it is the metaphor for "family" in social organization. Various *guanxi* networks govern different aspects of people's lives and define a person's identity.

In some sense, Weber's (1951) description of Chinese society as based on patrimonialism, in which a person's power lies in his relationship with the ruler, has not been reversed. Such can be seen in the findings of the persistent power of cadres and clientelist ties between the political elite and entrepreneurs in many studies in the market transition debate. Is it possible to have a capitalist market economy without a Western rational-legal system? Is *guanxi* something inherent in Chinese culture or the result of a specific institutional setting? Do *guanxi* and the market have an inverse relationship so that the increase of one will lead to the diminishing role of the other?

From Weber to Parsons and on to modernization theory, social scientists generally believe that in a market economy human relations will be more affective-neutral and rational. However, many observers also find that in Japan and the newly industrialized economies in East Asia – Taiwan, Hong Kong, Singapore, and South Korea – family and other kinship or pseudo-kinship ties play an important role in the development of a capitalist economy and may actually be conducive to economic efficiency. For example, Ronald Dore (1983: 459–482) describes the kind of "relational contracting" in Japan that is more long term and collective-oriented and based on mutual obligation rather than short-term profit maximization. For some, China's choice of development is rooted in its East Asian location and a large population of successful overseas Chinese entrepreneurs, which both stimulates its desire for economic growth and provides it with opportunities and resources, such as foreign direct investment, trade, and other exchanges (Li 1994; Walder 1996). China is, therefore, following the East Asian model: an authoritarian government supervising the market reforms or the so-called developmental state, an export-oriented economy, and more importantly, a cultural tradition that emphasizes collective solidarity, social relationships, achievement-oriented work ethic, and the prestige of education.

Although some scholars (Guthrie 2002; Hanser 2002) suggest that with the development of a market economy and an increasing emphasis on the "rule by law," the importance of *guanxi* and *guanxi* practices is declining. Others (Bian 2002a; Potter 2002), however, insist that guanxi still exerts great influence and such a force may be on the rise because of the institutional void created by the abandonment of the old state mechanisms, such as the job allocation system and the immaturity of new market and legal mechanisms. A similar view is expressed in what Boisot and Child (1996) call "network capitalism." In the absence of effective state planning and given traditional Chinese social organization, decentralization in governance leads not to markets but to clans and permits the more local and personalized institutional order.

Still others believe that guanxi relations can produce distinct effects in different organizations at various stages. For example, Bian (2002b), in his study of social capital and firm performance through a survey of 188 firms in Guangzhou, concludes that private and semiprivate firms in the tertiary sector have more social capital than state-owned firms. Peng and Luo (2000) differentiate the two types of managerial networks: ties with officials and ties with other firms. They suggest that in transitional economies connections with officials are more important than those with managers in other firms because firms may have greater resource dependence on officials than on their industrial partners.

Despite the cultural factors, as Bian and Potter correctly point out, guanxi can be a supplement to the incomplete and immature social and legal systems in a transitional economy. Take private enterprises as an example; they are less likely than their state counterparts to get loans in the formal loan market. Brandt and Li (2003), by studying the matched bank-firm data, find that both private enterprises and privatized collective enterprises are discriminated against by Chinese banks. They have more difficulties receiving loans, and when they do, they get smaller loans and are subject to higher standards, *ceteris paribus*. Such discrimination is not even the result of limited credit information, for the privatized township and village enterprises (TVE)[8] were as likely as other TVEs to receive loans prior to their ownership reform. There is also no evidence that private enterprises have a higher probability of default and are thus more risky,

---

[8]  Township and village enterprises marked the high point of rural industry in China during the 1980s when such employment surpassed agriculture as the dominant source of total rural income. Because of the substitution of the household contract responsibility system for collective farming in agriculture and rural industrialization through TVEs, the peasants' standard of living was substantially improved in the 1980s.

yet they do not get sufficient loans. Facing such an institutional environment, it is hardly surprising to see the use of personal ties, both family and kinship ties and connections with the government officials, to get the resources needed for these enterprises.

The growing economic sociology literature indicates that even in advanced capitalist countries social relations and market exchanges are always intertwined, and economic action is socially situated or embedded. The "impersonal" market transaction or the market as an autonomous entity disconnected from society thus only exists in economic models, not in social reality.[9] The question, therefore, is not so much about whether guanxi is cultural or institutional or whether it will rise or decline, but under what circumstances who uses what kind of ties, and how people mobilize guanxi to cope with and make sense of institutional change.

By reviewing the paradoxes in China's reforms, readers are probably left with the following impression of China: a growing market economy with a Communist Party-led state that still sees Marxism, socialism, Party leadership, and a people's democratic dictatorship as its fundamental principles; a seemingly strong state that nonetheless allows local variations and flexibility; and an increasingly capitalistic economy with the lingering power of guanxi still apparent. In the following chapters, I will discuss three industrialized villages – all among the ten wealthiest villages in China – and document how local communities improvise and innovate to deal with the economic transition and how they make sense of their lives and maintain their community identity during unprecedented social change.

In response to the market transition debate, I argue that changes in property rights (i.e., privatization) alone cannot explain the dynamics of social change in China, and it is the interaction between the larger economic and political institutions, together with local social, economic, and political resources, that determines which path of development local communities will embark on. I propose that the local institutional innovations may well provide alternatives to the sharp dichotomy between communism and capitalism, state and market. One of these possible alternatives is what I call "community capitalism," which combines market production and distribution with redistribution and the provision of public goods based on group boundaries.

---

[9]  See Mark Granovetter's seminal work in economic sociology, "Economic Action and Social Structure: The Problem of Embeddedness," *American Journal of Sociology*, 1985, 91: 481–510, and his more recent elaboration in "The Impact of Social Structure on Economic Outcomes," *Journal of Economic Perspectives*, 2005, 19 (1): 33–50.

## Community Capitalism

Community capitalism represents an alternative model of development for transitional societies.[10] Here, community is widely defined as a group with a commonly recognized identity, and group members more or less share common interests. In the three cases that I discuss later, they happen to be villages – the smallest local communities in rural China. Villages are not considered to be official administrative units but self-governing entities in China, although the Party-State does penetrate into them. Community capitalism mobilizes and organizes the economic, political, and social capital at the community level to compete for resources at the upper levels and in the global market. At the local level, it provides public goods and social welfare benefits, such as housing, education, and health care, to community members through redistribution. The model is sustained by common values and group boundaries created by community membership and family and pseudo-family networks, at the core of which are usually the village elite who have come into power.

Community capitalism is different from both traditional state socialism and prototypical capitalism. First of all, it is capitalist, as communities actively participate in the market and produce for profits. In fact, all of the three villages that I will discuss later are not only communities but also collectively owned corporations, and one of them has already been listed on the Shenzhen Stock Exchange. Second, the village government works as an executive board to distribute resources and welfare benefits and, at the same time, makes economic decisions and competes for resources from upper-level administrations on behalf of the villagers. As a result, community is both a unit of redistribution and an entity competing in the market. In addition, villages maintain collectivist values as a sense-making mechanism to justify the profit-driven activities, hold their members together, and sustain the model. To some extent, community capitalism is a capitalist form of economic arrangements without the introduction of the full set of capitalist values. Local states both guide and participate in economic activities, and traditional family values as well as the socialist legacies play an important role in providing a safety net for the villagers and achieving social cohesion.

Within the community, there can be different forms of distribution and systems of social and economic organization. It can be more like a

---

[10] See also my article "From Mao to the Market: Community Capitalism in Rural China," *Theory, Culture & Society*, 2011, 28(2): 46–68.

cooperative in which community members collectively own the means of production, produce together, and share the profits; however, it can also be a community where only certain resources are commonly owned and profits are partially shared. It can operate centrally or in a more dispersed manner, with the community leaders or households having greater autonomy. No matter whether more incomes are distributed according to labor, capital, or membership, some form of collectivism is kept to pool resources together and to provide members with a safety net.

## About the Book

Can communism and a market economy be made compatible? Theoretically, this raises a major problem: to most people's understanding, the market belongs to capitalism, which features competition and profit making, whereas communism has a completely different philosophy. In the early twenty-first century, communism seems to be extremely unfashionable, if not anachronistic, with the collapse of the Soviet Union, the transformation of former socialist countries in Eastern Europe, and the increasing development of markets and privatization in China, presently the largest "socialist" state in the world. However, empirically the question posed at the beginning is not entirely impossible, for even though it may be hard to practice communism in a market context on a large scale, it is much easier to have small communes emphasizing collective ownership and egalitarianism (such as Israeli kibbutzim and Yamagishi villages in Japan), although an increasingly globalized market makes any alternatives difficult to thrive.[11] At the rural grassroots level, a number of successful local communities in China retained collective ownership while performing adequately in the market, as revealed by the once booming TVEs.

Entering the 1990s, however, the halo over the TVEs lost its glamour, when growth of the enterprises and competition from product markets were beyond the control of local officials. As a result, many TVEs were privatized or evolved into mixed economies.[12] Nevertheless, some villages survived the wave of privatization and maintained their collective

---

[11] At its centenary the equalized cooperative form of the kibbutz movement, faced with a crisis in a market-driven globalized world, is gradually integrating a privatized model (see Harriet Sherwood, "The Kibbutz: 100 Years Old and Facing an Uncertain Future," *The Guardian*, August 13, 2010).

[12] For the changing property rights in rural China, see Jean Oi and Andrew Walder, eds., *Property Rights and Economic Reform in China* (Stanford, CA: Stanford University Press, 1999).

ownership of the enterprises. Nanjie Village, in northern China, was one of them. All the means of production in the village are owned collectively, and wealth is distributed on a relatively equal basis among all the villagers. In fact, the success of Nanjie Village has inspired some surrounding villages to re-collectivize and follow its example. Why does the village go against the popular trend? How does it manage to do so? These were the two questions that initially attracted me to this research.

However, it is not entirely the exceptional features of this village that caught my attention. The real value of the research is that this situation may not be exceptional – that is, this village may offer an alternative way of organizing production and distribution at this particular moment in history and may provide a lens through which we can more clearly view the complexity and reality of Chinese society. The reasons are as follows: (1) Nanjie does not have any special advantages, such as abundant natural resources or overseas connections, that differentiate it from other places; (2) it is located in a modestly developed area, if not an underdeveloped region, in China; (3) it seems to be capable of solving the problems facing most rural communities (e.g., poverty, lack of social welfare, and "peasant burdens"[13]) through its own policies and has attracted people from other places in China, which indicates the appeal of this form of development.

Development policies often involve a deep-rooted, anti-rural bias, as seen in the tradition of modernization theory, which suggests that the rural way of living is tied to backwardness while an urban lifestyle is considered to be

[13] Because village government is not an administrative level, its revenue and the income of the officials depend on the taxes and surcharges paid by peasants. When supervision is lacking, village governments can be very predatory and corrupt, adding various burdens on peasants. As a result, for some villages the tension between local governments and peasants is so intense that protests and other kinds of resistance occur. Peasant burdens have thus become a serious problem in rural China, and the central government is trying different ways to reduce the burdens. For descriptions of peasant life and peasant resistance, see Chen Guidi and ChunTao, *A Survey of Chinese Peasants (Zhongguo Nongmin Diaocha)*, 2004. Of course, since there has been a lot of rural discontent, the central government has, in recent years, made significant policy changes including the abolition of the agricultural tax, which is a lump-sum fee paid by peasants based on their amount of cultivated land and size of the household and often accounts for more than one-tenth of their annual income. Before the abolition, the agricultural tax revenue went to local governments. Removing agricultural tax has definitely improved the lives of those subsistence peasants, but it has also caused a reduction in local revenues and strains on the local governments' budget. Meanwhile, local governments have not become less predatory but are seeking other means to profiteer, such as through land appropriation, which has been the leading cause of local disputes in recent years. For example, in September 2011 villagers in Wukan in Guangdong province protested against the village government's land seizures, and the protests escalated into an uprising in December (see Andrew Jacobs, "Village Revolts Over Inequalities of Chinese Life," *The New York Times*, December 14, 2011).

a more advanced, modern trait. Since the Enclosure Movement in England, dismantling the peasantry seems to have been, as Polanyi ([1944] 1957) suggests, both a precondition for and a result of the expansion of market relations. It is thus generally believed, based on Western experience, that peasants will become marginalized as a country becomes modernized and industrialized while subsistence farming will be replaced by large mechanized farms owned by capitalist farmers or agribusinesses. In China, people can witness a similar trend of displaced peasants looking for low-wage jobs in the cities and abandoning subsistence farming that is no longer viable as a result of reforms. The difference is that land is still collectively owned in rural China, and it is thus possible, although not easy, for rural communities with good organization to maintain their vitality.

Since the Maoist era, China has adopted a very unbalanced development strategy in favor of those living in towns and cities. Even the introduction of the "household responsibility system" to rural areas at the beginning of the reform era, a supposedly more radical reform policy, has not enabled peasants to achieve long-term prosperity. However, until 2012, the majority of the Chinese population had been rural,[14] so rural issues including how to mitigate the brunt of marketization and urbanization borne by peasants were significant in their own right. From collectivization in Maoist China to de-collectivization in post-Mao China, from the boom of household farming and TVEs to the doom of urban bias in development, peasants have experienced the changes from high political status, although often nominal, to substantial economic achievements and finally to relative poverty and little political power. Therefore, it is intriguing to see how local rural communities interact with state policies, seeking their way to both economic prosperity and social solidarity.

The reasons peasants are an underprivileged group in China are complicated – many are historical and related to cultural traditions – but here I will review some of the institutional constraints.

In a sense, the problems facing rural China are embedded in the political-institutional structure. Montinola, Qian, and Weingast call the Chinese political system "federalism, Chinese style" (1995), and Oi describes rural governments as "local state corporatism" (1999). On the one hand,

---

[14] According to the *China Statistical Yearbook 2009 (zhongguo tongji nianjian 2009)*, as of 2008, China's rural population still accounted for 54% of the total population, that is, more than 721 million people. The National Bureau of Statistics announced in January 2012 that China had, for the first time ever, more urban than rural dwellers. Urban residents now account for 51.27% of the entire population, yet there are still more than 650 million rural residents.

because of the decentralization and fiscal reforms, local governments have more discretion over their own economic development and more incentives and also pressure to pursue economic growth to increase their revenues. On the other hand, the central government is still the major policy maker, and there are always quotas set for local governments to meet. Therefore, the power of local governments is restrained by fixed quotas yet without substantial supervision over how these are to be met or whether they are possible to achieve. Even if the central government has the intention of improving the peasants' lives, it is hard for the central state to get a precise picture of the real situation in different areas of rural China. Similarly, because policies have to pass through so many administrative levels, they are difficult to implement without any distortion.[15] Moreover, because of the whole cadre promotion system,[16] local cadres often do not need to be accountable to peasants but only to their superiors to get promoted; they do not have to substantially improve peasants' lives but only need to build several "face projects" that are often oriented toward the short term.

As a result of this combination of command and market forces, rural policies are sometimes made out of good or even idealistic intentions yet lack practical value. Local governments, whether they want it or not, are often accused of levying heavy burdens on peasants and of corruption and abuse. For example, since the central government abolished the agricultural tax in 2005, which was meant to reduce burdens on peasants, land disputes have become a major source of tension at local levels, as cadres appropriate land from peasants for real estate development and other commercial uses to boost local revenues and sometimes their personal pockets. To balance state interests and parochial interests, peasants' interests and administrative interests, the distortion of central policies is not a rare phenomenon, which can either lead to innovation and experiments in new patterns of reform or give rise to tensions between the peasants and local authorities. Several studies indicate that peasants tend to trust the central government more than its local representatives.[17]

---

[15] Xueguang Zhou (2008) expresses similar views in his article on collusion among different levels of local governments to cope with central commands as a result of the distance separating central policies and local realities and the common interests among local states.

[16] For a detailed discussion of the cadre evaluation system, see Susan Whiting, *Power and Wealth in Rural China: The Political Economy of Institutional Change* (Cambridge: Cambridge University Press, 2001), and Maria Edin, "State Capacity and Local Agent Control in China: CCP Cadre Management from a Township Perspective," *The China Quarterly*, 2003, 173: 35–52.

[17] See, for example, Lianjiang Li, "Political Trust in Rural China," *Modern China*, 2004, 30(2): 228–258.

From a social perspective, this is the result of the rural-urban divide. This division of the population, together with the *hukou* system, deprives the rural people of health care, education, housing, employment, and other social welfare benefits enjoyed by those living in towns and cities.[18] Especially since the late 1990s, as the Chinese central government has been focusing on modernization (including urbanization and industrialization) and globalization, cities have received more attention and support from the state. In contrast, the surplus labor in rural China has become the largest floating population in the world, creating millions of migrant workers or peasant workers (*nongmin gong*) who work in urban factories and contribute to the sustained gross domestic product (GDP) growth of the country, yet do not enjoy urban *hukou* and the status and benefits attached to it.

Because of this division along rural-urban residence, both migration and social mobility are restricted. Without much social capital, the rural population became the most disadvantaged and vulnerable group in the process of modernization. Politically, they do not have any bargaining power in policy making. Socially, there are not many associations mobilizing and organizing them to fight for their rights, especially with weakening labor unions in reform-era China that are often more pro-business than pro-labor. Furthermore, they are on average less educated than the urban population and lack useful social networks to move up the social ladder. Economically, their income is far below that of the urban population, and they are almost always excluded from the privileged jobs occupied by urbanites. Many of them are working on or below minimum wages and with little social security.

In addition, the severity of the problem varies across regions. As a result of different natural conditions, historical backgrounds, economic resources, political constraints, and the skills of local leadership, some rural areas are more developed and wealthier than others. Some regions are still largely based on agriculture; others are gradually industrializing. The coastal areas, especially villages in Guangdong province, have more foreign-capital enterprises or joint ventures and greater contacts with foreign countries and the

---

[18] Of course, with the privatization of health care, housing, and other welfare benefits in cities, many urban residents have also started to suffer from the lack of affordable social services, but the situation in rural China is more severe and has a longer history. For *hukou* and migrant workers, see Dorothy Solinger's *Contesting Citizenship in Urban China: Peasant Migrants, the State, and the Logic of the Market.* (Berkeley and Los Angeles, CA: University of California Press, 1999).

international market.[19] Some localities lead the rural reform, while others learn and imitate. Local people, in varying degrees, are able to create different ways of adaptation to the larger political and social environment using the resources available to them.

With this theoretical introduction completed, the following chapters will discuss the institutional innovations in three rural communities – Nanjie Village, Huaxi Village, and Shangyuan Village – as they cope with the dual transition from a planned economy to a market economy and from an agrarian society to an industrialized society and strive for both economic prosperity and social solidarity.

In Chapter 2, I analyze the case of Nanjie Village in Henan province, central China. The village has adopted a strategy encapsulated by the slogan "circle on the outside and square on the inside" (*waiyuan neifang*). In contrast to the large-scale privatization taking place in China, Nanjie Village maintains its collective ownership and many of the characteristic features of the Maoist era, such as singing revolutionary songs and reciting from the "Red Bible." Meanwhile, the village has, over the past three decades, developed dozens of collectively owned and operated factories and companies ranging from food processing to pharmaceuticals and has thus been able to provide its villagers with better social welfare than most other rural communities in China.

The next case study, explored in Chapter 3, discusses Huaxi Village in Jiangsu province, one of the representatives of the well-known *Sunan* or Southern Jiangsu model, and now the wealthiest village in China. The village's economic performance and living conditions surpass many cities in China and even in the United States. By 2005 the village's total industrial output had exceeded 24.5 billion yuan (about US$3 billion using the 2005 exchange rate) (Lu 2006), and the average annual income had reached 35,002 yuan per capita (about US$4,300) (ibid.). While the once booming TVEs have been largely privatized since the 1990s, Huaxi has stayed on its path with the innovation of a property system in which each villager becomes a shareholder in the collective enterprises.

The final variant can be found in the case of Shangyuan Village located in Wenzhou city, Zhejiang province, a place known for its prosperous family

---

[19] Because of its geographic location, Guangdong province has many international contacts. Some areas, like Kaiping County, have many emigrant villages (*qiaoxiang*) with a large proportion of the population migrating to other countries, and those who stay rely on remittances from abroad to buy luxuries or to open their own businesses.

businesses and hard-working private entrepreneurs. Despite its thriving private economy, Shangyuan Village retains a collective control over the use of land, something similar to a shareholding land cooperative. The village developed several commercial clusters including a low-voltage electrical equipment market and a nonferrous metal market and distributes dividends to the villagers from the rent collected. In this way, villagers are guaranteed a minimum income, housing, and a storefront (*dianmian*). Meanwhile, because of those marketplaces, the booming housing price supplies the villagers with extra economic benefits. As a result, while competing in the market, private entrepreneurs are provided with a safety net sustained by the collective use of the land.

In the concluding chapter, I compare and contrast the three villages along the axes of ownership structures, institutions, and culture and social networks. I then discuss the rationality of collectivism and how community capitalism works as an alternative model of development. Thus, the whole study presents a set of viable routes to rural development with profound implications for China and the rest of the developing world.

Finally, I want to explain why I selected these three villages. First, some of the people would ask why I picked three rich, highly industrialized, and therefore "non-typical" villages rather than those poverty-stricken villages in the hinterland. I would argue that exactly because the three villages are all model villages in China they offer good cases for studying how the rural economy actually works. The lessons we can draw from successful stories are not any less than those from failed experiences. Second, the three villages demonstrate different mixes along the organizational continuum from market economy to collectivism. Behind the common economic success, what makes these villages different? How did they come up with the way in which they organized themselves? The three villages constitute a good comparison. Third, they are located in different regions with distinct natural conditions and historical backgrounds, which can make the story more generalizable, because they represent three possible trends in China's transition that exhibit a balance between the state and the market and capitalism and socialism, and combine competition with cooperation.

Scholars have diverse views on whether collective land ownership or state intervention is necessary for rural development. Those who favor the power of the market argue that land privatization and a free market are the solutions to peasant issues in China as they create efficiency and release entrepreneurship that can improve the lives of peasants and better protect their rights (Yang 2001; Wu 2002; Dang 2007). Critics argue that land privatization is dangerous and can create a large number of landless and jobless peasants as land will get concentrated into a few hands. Furthermore, cities cannot absorb so many surplus laborers, thus widening the gap between the rich and the poor and further marginalizing peasants (Wen 2008; Cao 2009; He 2010). For them, state intervention is both necessary and justified to protect peasants' basic rights, to invest in public goods, and to offer financial credit – all crucial for agricultural production.

Others, while generally agreeing with the current Chinese land system of collective land ownership and individualized land use rights, try to mitigate the two divided views, although the prescriptions they give diverge. Philip C.C. Huang (Huang Zongzhi), for example, proposes an end to the left-right divide and the start of a third path that goes beyond both ideologies and combines the best of the market and the state. He (2007; 2010) suggests that small family-based farms with peasants organizing themselves into voluntary agricultural associations are a better solution for China than big farms and agribusinesses in the West and the old collective farms that are directly controlled by the state. Zhang and Donaldson (2008) on the other hand, by studying vertically integrated agribusinesses in Shandong and Yunnan, suggest that the unique land institution in China protects agricultural producers from dispossession by external capital. However, it is also flexible enough for enhanced production needed by agribusinesses, and as a result, China is able to modernize its agriculture and expand its agricultural production without displacing the peasants by maintaining the current land institution while allowing for different forms of agribusinesses.

In the three villages that I study, agriculture is no longer the major source of income. They offer cases of how land ownership, the local state as well as the form of social organization affect rural industrialization. I agree with the critics of the neoliberal approach that a certain level of collectivization is important in rural development and that the state needs to provide basic services and public goods. However, in contrast to both private ownership and the traditional People's Commune's system, I believe that much autonomy should be delegated to local communities. Cui Zhiyuan (1993) proposes a similar view when he discusses the Moebius-strip collective ownership as the basis for rural industry, because it combines the interests of inside workers and outside community members. Cui (2005) advocates a kind of liberal socialism or petty bourgeois socialism in China based on shareholding cooperatives and social dividends, which combines competition with cooperation and creates a true type of market socialism. My cases also demonstrate some explorations on that front, but the mechanisms of production and distribution and the relationships between the local state and community members, as well as between insiders and outsiders, are much more complex. They indicate the dialectics between capitalism and communism, and between the state and the market. Therefore, I conceptualize it as community capitalism.

Of course, given the size and diversity of China, these three cases hardly cover all the hybrid forms, but I hope to present a China that has nothing to do with the big metropolises, a "monolithic" communist state, or unrelenting economic growth but with ordinary peasants in local communities looking to prosper in the midst of the state, the market, and a changing culture and society. All three villages' developmental strategies display the interaction between larger social and political institutions and their local conditions. Although the particular form of organization may not be replicable elsewhere, as conditions such as leadership, history, and geographic location are different, the way they cope with social change and the experience of exploring their respective path of development can be shared.

# TWO

# Circle on the Outside, Square on the Inside

Happiness is not the same as being rich, but being rich is part of happiness.
Wang Hongbin, Nanjie Party Secretary

In 1978, when a group of peasants from Xiaogang Village, located within Anhui province in southeast China, secretly signed a contract among themselves to divide the collective village farmland and start growing crops in household units, nobody expected that it could cause a national de collectivization of the communes and bring about the final establishment of a new economic institution – the household contract responsibility system – throughout China. Equally, few would have anticipated that two decades later, the same village that stirred up the turmoil to divide the communes in the late 1970s would fail to benefit much from its pioneering act and, in the face of a stagnant economy and deteriorating public goods and services, would decide to return to what it was originally against – collectivization. This time a once backward village in northern China became Xiaogang's role model, and this was Nanjie Village.[1]

## A Historical Dialectic:
## Collectivization–De-collectivization–Re-collectivization

Nanjie Village (or South Street Village), a settlement with an area of less than two square kilometers comprising some 850 households with a population of slightly more than 3,000 individuals, is located in the central part of Henan province in northern China, from where the traditional Chinese

---

[1] For a report on Xiaogang Village's development after 1978, see Xian Ye, "Xiaogangcun 'Dabaogan' 30 Nian" (30 Years of the Contract System in Xiaogang Village), *Zhongguo Baodao* (*China Report*), 2008, 2: 63–66.

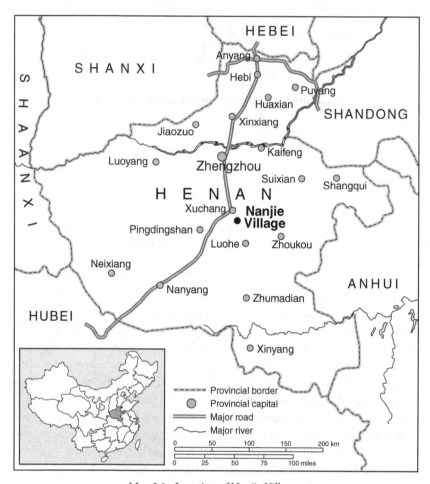

Map 2.1.  Location of Nanjie Village.

agrarian culture originates (Map 2.1). There are five administrative levels above the village – that is, the central government, Henan provincial government, Luohe municipal government, Linying county government, and Chengguan township government, although as a result of its outstanding economic and political status within the province, the village often deals directly with the county government, skipping the township level. Wang Hongbin, the village party secretary, is also deputy chairman of the Standing Committee of Luohe Municipal People's Congress.

To this day, Henan province has not been as rich and developed as the coastal provinces despite its longer history of civilization, and agriculture has remained the major source of income for much of the rural area in Henan. Nanjie Village, however, is somewhat different from other villages in the province in that it is rich and highly industrialized and more distinctively "red" – communist red. The village still has about 1,000 mu (roughly 165 acres) of arable farmland, and the rest of the land has been transformed into housing and industrial zones. Villagers enjoy a comprehensive social welfare system. People call it a collage of Maoist ideology and an economic miracle, a village still in the Mao era,[2] a "communist theme park,"[3] or "a red village with hundreds of millions of *yuan*" as Nanjie villagers describe themselves on their Web site.[4]

There have been no complete village histories so far. When I was there in early 2006, the director of the Village Archives, Mr. Wang, told me that they had just started compiling the village history of which he was in charge. They chose people from each factory to write a part. Because many people who had witnessed the changes of the village passed away, and they needed to collect a lot of archival materials and to conduct many interviews, the whole work was progressing rather slowly.[5] I was lucky to find that the room for the village history compiling team was right next to Lü Xiaohu's office,[6] the secretary of the Village Youth League Committee and one of my key contacts. Mr. Lü and I found several handwritten and typed draft chapters on the desks, allowing me to read and take notes of some of the important information.

The draft chapters mostly cover events from the 1950s until August 1991. During these years, China had experienced, as a nation, many turning points in its development, including the incessant political mobilizations and mass movements in the Maoist era and the economic and political

---

[2]  See Francis Markus's report, "Chinese Village Still in Mao Era" at BBC news on Nov. 19, 2002 (http://news.bbc.co.uk/2/hi/asia-pacific/2488905.stm); Erik Eckholm's story "Detour on Capitalist Road: Diehard Maoist Collective" (*New York Times*, Jan. 7, 1999) and Anthony Spaeth's story "Back to the Future" (*Time*, Feb. 5, 1996).

[3]  See Todd Crowell and Anne Naham's article, "A Communist Theme Park" (*Asiaweek*, Jan. 22, 1999).

[4]  Nanjie Village has built a Web site promoting its economic development and ideology. The address is http://www.nanjiecun.cn.

[5]  In the summer of 2006, I interviewed the two people who were in charge of compiling the village history; both were retired cadres from the county. At the time, they estimated that the project would be complete in October and promised to mail a copy to me when it was available. Qu Yuhong emailed me a few draft chapters later. When I asked again about the village history in the summer of 2010, I was told that Nanjie had stopped the compilation. I received a copy of the village history that is for internal circulation only in the summer of 2011.

[6]  As of 2010, Lü Xiaohu had left the Youth League and was in charge of tourism in Nanjie.

transformation during the period of reform. Along with several publications on the village, the *History of Linying County (Linying Xianzhi)*, and the oral history of the elderly in the village,[7] I was able to get a sense of what had taken place over these years. I have no intention to recapitulate the history of socialist China, or even the village history here, but it is necessary to sketch an outline of the important events from the 1950s to the 1990s to provide the context for this study.

Nanjie covers the southern area of the central region of Linying county, hence the name Nanjie, meaning south street in Chinese. In the Sui dynasty (AD 581–618), a flood destroyed the old center of the county, so the government moved south to the site of today's Chengguan town, where Nanjie is located. Nanjie Village was thus formed in a rather different manner from most other natural villages (*zirancun*, meaning "spontaneously formed rural settlements"). Villagers considered themselves to be urban residents (*chengliren*). Since 1949 people who lived in the four streets of the county center, as long as they chose to receive an allotment of land, were all classified as rural residents in China's modern household registration system, which is, according to Mr. Wang, distinct from many other areas where in similar circumstances people are usually registered as urban residents.[8] Because of its closeness to town, villagers in Nanjie have a tradition of operating small businesses and getting involved in commerce in addition to farming.

After the Chinese Communist Party took over China in 1949, it redistributed the formerly concentrated land to families on a per capita basis. Even peasants who previously did not have any land got their share. However, to solidify the land reform, prevent any backlash from the landlords, and manage labor – the most abundant resource – in a more effective and egalitarian way, collectivization was imposed in rural China.

In 1950, following Chairman Mao's call for advancing production by better organization (*zuzhi qilai, fazhan shengchan*), Linying county established an agricultural mutual aid and cooperation office (*nongye huzhu hezuo bangongshi*). This led to the formation of the first mutual aid team in the county in 1951. The mutual aid team is a low-level form of collectivization

---

[7] I held a group interview with five elderlies in the village on February 16, 2006.

[8] The modern household registration (*hukou*) system in China officially started in 1958, which aimed to restrict people's mobility and migration. It is difficult for rural people to move to cities and for people from small cities to get into big cities, and many privileges and supplies are attached to urban *hukou*, such as education, health care, employment, etc. To date, although the whole system has been relaxed, it still plays an important role in people's social and economic lives. It is, for example, extremely hard to get a Beijing or Shanghai *hukou*.

so that each wealthier family can help several poor families improve their agricultural skills and thus better their economic conditions. In this form, people in the team only pool their labor in farming, while the outputs are distributed according to one's area of land, and land and tools are still individually owned. By the end of 1953, there were more than 9,800 mutual aid teams, and about 65 percent of the households in Linying county joined such groups (Li 1996). In 1954, Nanjie Village formed its own mutual aid teams. A year later, about 85 percent of the households in Linying joined the low-level agricultural cooperatives (*diji nongye hezuoshe*) (ibid.), where peasants not only farmed together but also pooled their farming tools, draft animals, and land as their equity contribution. People were paid in accordance with their labor input and the size of their land.

However, such cooperatives were still small in scale, usually consisting of twenty to thirty families. By January 1956, Juling Agricultural Cooperative, the first high-level cooperative (*gaoji hezuoshe*), was formed in Linying, and more than 300 peasants participated in it. The head of the second such organization in the county, Zang Baoxuan, was the neighbor of Wang Hongbin who has been Nanjie's party secretary since 1977. The two cooperatives were the demonstration sites in the county at the time. All the farming tools and draft animals were sold to the co-ops and owned collectively, which marked the completion of the socialist transformation (*shehui zhuyi gaizao*). The same year, virtually all households in Linying joined the high-level cooperatives, which usually consisted of around 200 families.

In 1958, collectivization became even more radical; high-level cooperatives were combined into communes. The ten towns in the county formed ten people's communes (*renmin gongshe*), including Chengguan Commune in which Nanjie was one of the eighteen production brigades.[9] All the land, assets, tools, draft animals, crops, and even the previously allowed private plots were taken over by the communes to manage and distribute in an absolutely egalitarian way. Meanwhile, communal dining halls were built for members to get food according to their needs, and people no longer cooked for themselves, thus appeared the so-called communal pot or *daguofan*. Under this system, villages became production brigades (*shengchan dadui*), and mutual aid teams became production teams or platoons (*shengchan dui*).

---

[9] The people's communes were formerly the highest of three administrative levels in rural areas during the period from 1958 to the early 1980s until they were replaced by townships. Communes, the largest collective units, were divided into production brigades and production teams. Communes became an official state policy in 1958 after Mao Zedong's visit to an unofficial commune in Henan province.

However, these changes produced production units that were too large to manage, and many peasants lost their motivation in the excessive egalitarianism of the movement. The free rider problem, which was compounded by cadres' lying and exaggerating about the local achievements, together with a series of natural disasters, resulted in China being caught in a quagmire of starvation and economic recession. In 1962, the central government adjusted the commune system. The ownership of the means of production was shared by the three administrative levels – communes, production brigades, and production teams – and the teams became the basic unit for accounting, operation, and management (*sanji suoyou, dui wei jichu*). The communal dining halls were also abandoned, and families got back their private plots as a source of extra income.

During the Cultural Revolution from 1966 to 1976, all the family and private businesses were banned as capitalist endeavors. The popular local family restaurants were shut down in Nanjie, such as Guo's Bistro renowned for its spicy pepper soup (*hula tang*, a specialty in Henan cuisine) and the Hui[10] people's beef dumpling (*guotie*) restaurants. To this point, Nanjie's history was not that distinct from thousands of other villages in China, and, according to the elderly, Nanjie was quite backward in terms of agricultural production in the 1960s. Used to running small businesses, the villagers had a hard time adapting to their lives as farming peasants.

However, while in 1978 peasants in Xiaogang Village first started the practice of household responsibility, Nanjie Village did not complete its de-collectivization until 1982.[11] At this time, most of China had already caught up with the new practice, and according to the *History of Linying County* (Li 1996: 290), "the household responsibility system was universally adopted throughout the county" by 1982. Several elderly villagers told me that the reason Nanjie was almost the last to de-collectivize in the county was because the then party secretary, having observed other de-collectivized villages, thought that such a strategy was not a viable solution and thus

---

[10] The Hui are China's Han Muslim minority. For an ethnic study of Hui Muslims, see Xiaowei Zang, *Ethnicity and Urban Life in China: A Comparative Study of Hui Muslims and Han Chinese* (New York: Routledge, 2007). For a review article on China's ethnic relations between Muslims and Han, see Xiaoshuo Hou and John Stone, "The Ethnic Dilemma in China's Industrial Revolution," *Ethnic and Racial Studies*, 2008, 31(4): 812–817.

[11] In the interviews with some village administrators who are not Nanjie natives and in some newspaper stories, it was also claimed that Nanjie adopted the household responsibility system and divided the land in 1981 and re-collectivized in 1984. However, here I took the timeline from the draft chapters of the village history and the elderlies' accounts that Nanjie completed its land division in 1982 and re-collectivized in 1986, and the years were also confirmed in the internally circulated *Village History* I received in 2011.

refused to contract out the land. It was not until 1982, in the face of pressure from above, that Nanjie started to divide land and distribute it to households, but the brigade also proposed that contract land should not be too scattered. To support efficient household farming, each household's allocation of land should, in general, not exceed three plots, and the quality of land was also taken into consideration.

De-collectivization did not bring about advances in agricultural production. Mr. Li, one of the elderlies in the village, explained:

At that time agricultural machines were very large, not suitable for small plots, so we still relied heavily on labor and draft animals. Households that had enough labor did pretty well after the land was divided, but for those who did not have enough labor, production volume dropped dramatically. In Nanjie, there were just too many people and too little land to divide. On average each person only had 0.7 *mu* [1/10 of an acre] of farmland. Deducting the grain given to the state, there were some 60 *jin* [30 kilograms] of wheat left for each household. The harvest of wheat was about 80 to 100 *jin* each harvest season, and there were two harvest seasons, usually a better harvest in the fall. To make up the shortage, we had to eat yams or dried yams, and later also corn. The number 12 and 13 were Hui brigades. Many of them had small businesses to supplement their livings. Those who ran businesses in addition to farming led better lives.

The relaxation of national policies on the rural economy provided peasants with new ways to get rich. Resurrecting their entrepreneurial traditions, many Nanjie people abandoned their farmland and set up food stalls or retail stores, and some even opened their own factories through partnerships with their families or friends. Therefore, people had fewer incentives to take care of their land, reducing their investment in agriculture or even contracting out their farms to relatives or friends. Mr. Duan, director of the Party Committee Office, described the situation at the time:

After dividing up the land, people all left for cities to find jobs, except for old people and small children. Nobody wanted to stay farming. Land was abandoned. At that time, there was an article in *The People's Daily* entitled "Who will Till the Peasants' Land?," saying that industries should give back to agriculture just as agriculture had previously always supported industries, and peasant workers should be encouraged to stay in their villages to find jobs. Meanwhile, the Village Party Committee was no longer capable of mobilizing the peasants; they wouldn't listen to the Party any more.

In 1986, following the directive from the central government that villages suitable for collectivization could go ahead, and those suitable for de-collectivization should move in the opposite direction (*yi tong ze tong, yi fen ze fen*), the Nanjie Village Party Committee put up a poster instructing villagers that all who were capable of farming should take care of their contract land first before starting businesses; otherwise, the Party Committee had the right to intervene. Farmland was not allowed to be abandoned or contracted out to non-villagers. Peasants who had specific reasons for not being able to farm the land could submit an application to the Village Party Committee to entrust their land to the village for collective farming, and the village would in turn provide each person with a ration of flour – the staple food in northern China – on a monthly basis at a nominal price.[12] This ensured the livelihood of those who chose to turn their contract farmland back to the village. They could also get jobs at the village factories to enjoy stable salaries, which was extremely attractive to families who lacked labor and farming tools and those with too many family members to feed.

However, it was not just because of the concern for agricultural development that Nanjie wanted to re-collectivize its land use. In 1979 and 1980, Nanjie founded two village factories, which were quite successful. At that time, its industrial output almost equaled agricultural production (Liu 2004). With the land divided, those two collectively owned factories were also contracted out to individuals, which caused tension that I will discuss later. The point is that the Village Party Committee decided to run the factories again, and the expansion of collective enterprises needed land.

After reading the poster, 300 people submitted their applications to fill this need, among whom 100 were approved by the Party Committee and their land was taken over by the village that year. In 1987, the Village Agricultural Machinery Team that had been dismissed was reassembled to farm the collective land. By the end of 1990, all the villagers voluntarily[13] handed their farmland over to the village for collective farming. When asked whether there was any opposition during the re-collectivization of land, the elderly told me that at first there certainly was. However, later on, because the individual production volume was much smaller than that of

---

[12] The village provided each villager with 40 jin or 20 kilograms of flour every month at 0.18 yuan, roughly US$0.05 (based on the 1986 exchange rate), per jin, in exchange for the use right of their land. According to the database at the Web site of the Food and Agriculture Organization of the United Nations (http://faostat.fao.org), on a national level, China's per capita supply of wheat was 79.4 kilograms per year in 1986. Although annual statistics on the price and supply of flour were not available, I found in the database of China's Ministry of Agriculture that in 1986 the state purchasing price of wheat was set at 0.43 yuan, roughly US$0.12, per jin, and the negotiated price was 0.51 yuan, roughly US$0.15, per jin; both prices were supposed to be below the market price (http://www.agri.gov.cn/sjzl/baipsh/WB2001.htm#15) but were still much higher than the price Nanjie villagers got for their flour.

[13] Because at that time dividing land was still the trend, to have proof that the re-collectivization of land was not forced upon the villagers in case the state questioned it, each villager had to write an application and fingerprint it.

the collective, and the collective was better equipped with farm machinery, people all turned in their land.

In the immediate years after 1949, Nanjie had 2,376 mu (380 acres) of arable farmland. After forty years of changes in administrative units and land ownership, Nanjie had 2,006 mu (330 acres) of arable farmland by the end of 1991. Since the late 1990s, Nanjie only has about 1,000 mu of farmland, and a professional Agricultural Machinery Team of seventy people works on this collective farm, and they get paid in the form of a monthly salary, just like factory workers. Highly mechanized farming releases peasants from the tedious life of traditional cultivation so that they can work in the village factories; on the other hand, various agricultural taxes have never burdened Nanjie villagers, for the village pays them on behalf of every villager to the different administrative levels. Land re-collectivization was the first step of Nanjie's industrialization. It granted Nanjie possibilities to consolidate the parcelized land for collective enterprises. To a certain extent, this is the application of the economies of scale to land utilization. In areas where arable land is extremely limited and the population is dense, the amount each household can derive from farming their own plot is not sufficient and no other uses of land are possible because of the small size. Therefore, people tend to either form their own cooperatives or, with a strong local government, turn in their land to the village in exchange for food and/or social welfare.

## Industrialization: The Way to Get Rich

Chairman Mao used to dream about building his communist utopia in China, and one of the objectives he set in the 1950s was to allow every person, especially the peasants, to enjoy living in an apartment building with lights and telephones (*loushang louxia, diandeng dianhua*). It was a dream of a modernized China where poverty would be eradicated and everyone would live a happy life. Today that dream may seem to be a joke, for science and technology have moved the world in a direction that is far more advanced than people in the past could imagine. However, for many people in rural China, that is a goal that is not so remote. One day on the road to Nanjie, the driver made an interesting comment that Nanjie has fulfilled Chairman Mao's dream of *loushang louxia, diandeng dianhua*. Economically speaking, the village has definitely proved that collectivism can achieve more than what Mao expected (Map 2.2).

Walder and Oi (1999) suggest that there are two patterns that describe the role of local governments in economic activities. The first

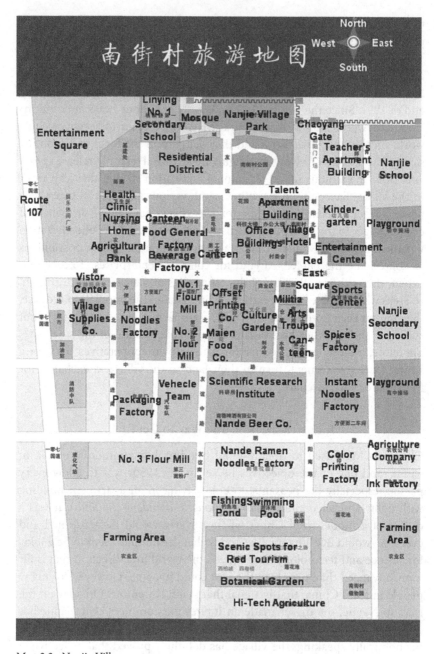

Map 2.2. Nanjie Village map.
*Source*: Nanjie Village Web site, http://nanjiecun.cn/hsly.asp?id=10, translated by the author.

one is "government-centered, in which village and township officials played an active entrepreneurial role, and industrial enterprises were government-owned.... This is the pattern of rural industrialization that has so often been referred to as a form of 'corporatism.'" The second approach is "entrepreneur-centered, and rural officials are not involved ... in the way that is typical of the corporate pattern ... and rural officials subsequently primarily played a supporting role in facilitating investment and growth in private enterprises." They call it the "littoral" pattern (p. 13). Walder and Oi point out that the two patterns are not static: The littoral regions evolved into shareholding cooperatives to mobilize government investment and seek official support. In the "corporatist" regions, public property is transformed by cadre elites either into an asset that "takes on the features of family property" or into investment in the private sector (p. 17).

In either case, local governments play a decisive role in rural industrialization; their willingness to reform and the means they choose can determine the type of development in a particular area. In the corporatist model, local governments mobilize and organize resources for industrialization on behalf of the villagers, and peasants are transformed into workers and shareholders of the collective enterprises. In the littoral model, peasants have to resort to their own resources, and they either become the floating population in cities, the so-called migrant workers, or turn into private entrepreneurs or their employees, depending on whether the local governments will provide any organizational resources. According to Walder and Oi's framework, Nanjie Village would belong to the corporatist pattern, in which the whole village is a legal entity with six corporations (including food, packaging and printing, small electrical appliances and artifacts, pharmaceuticals, real estates, and tourism) overseeing about twenty-six enterprises under its jurisdiction. Nanjie Village has also opened factories in other provinces such as Hubei and Gansu.

The path of Nanjie is in many aspects no different from other corporatist cases. Similar to Daqiuzhuang Village, which became Daqiuzhuang Town after November 1993, before Yu Zuomin's incarceration,[14] and Huaxi

---

[14] Daqiuzhuang, located in Tianjin, northern China, was once a legendary village that was transformed from a poor, barren land into one of the richest and most industrialized villages in China under the leadership of Yu Zuomin. Yu was the village's party secretary from 1974 to 1993 when he was imprisoned on the basis of the crimes of unlawful detention, offering bribes, concealing murderers, and interfering with the course of justice. He died of a heart attack in 1999 in the hospital. For Yu Zuomin's biography, consult Daqiuzhuang's official Web site, http://www.dqz.gov.cn/rdzt/yzm.htm.

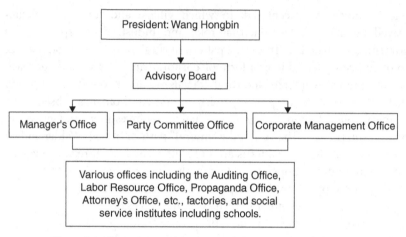

Figure 2.1. Organizational structure of Nanjie Corporate Group.

Village in Jiangsu province,[15] the local government in Nanjie is also the economic actor, and cadres are both political leaders and entrepreneurs who are responsible for economic decision making. To use many of my interviewees' own words, the relationship between the Party Committee and the corporate group is "two entities, one leadership (*liangkuai paizi, yitao renma*)," or expressed in the official discourse, "the manager responsibility system under the leadership of the Party Committee" (see Figure 2.1 for Nanjie's organizational structure).

Nanjie is often considered an economy led by capable persons (*nengren jingji*), although how to define "capable" is problematic. In the transitional period, leaders who have the guts, intelligence, political acumen, and networks and who are willing to help the peasants "get rich"[16] together can be of great value to local development, especially at the outset. Wang Hongbin is not only the party secretary of Nanjie Village, but also deputy chairman of the Standing Committee of the Luohe Municipal People's Congress, and used to be the deputy party secretary of Linying county – a person who has built up his political networks and power. He has been the number one figure in Nanjie since 1977 and is highly respected in the village. The villagers

---

[15] Huaxi Village is another star village in China with very successful village-owned enterprises. I will discuss it in detail in the next chapter.

[16] Deng Xiaoping, the designer and leader of the Chinese reform movement, proposed that "to get rich is glorious" and said that China should allow, or even encourage, some people to get rich first before common prosperity is achieved.

call him Squad Leader (*banzhang*), and many take him as their role model. As a Nanjie native, he gave up his job at a factory in the county to return to Nanjie to be a peasant in 1974 and led his production team to become a model team whose wheat output increased by 200 percent in two years. In 1976 he joined the Communist Party. As the leader of a billion dollar corporation and a well-known village, he still lives a simple life, earning 250 yuan (about US$37) a month and never receiving any bonuses. His charisma and discipline are clearly important reasons why villagers trust and follow him.

Nanjie's leadership includes Party, village, and corporate leaders (*sanda banzi*) – altogether twenty-one people, nine of whom are the Village Party Committee members forming the core of the leadership. There are four deputy party secretaries in charge of accounting, the Villagers' Committee (who is also the village head), joint ventures and public relations, and the militia, respectively. In addition, the leadership includes the directors of offices such as the Corporate Management Office, Accounting Office, Labor Resource Office, Utilities Office, and two deputy directors of the Villagers' Committee.

From a national perspective, in the 1980s, township and village enterprises were prevalent and collective ownership was common; however, entering the 1990s, privatization started to take place and privately owned enterprises became more dominant. For Nanjie Village, however, both agricultural and nonagricultural segments are under collective ownership; all the means of production and the majority of the remaining resources are collectively owned and distributed.

Nanjie Village used to be a very poor village. People called it *nanjiecun*, meaning a difficult or backward village, which has the same pronunciation as Nanjie Village in Chinese but is spelled with different characters. By 1976, the only nonagricultural asset in the village was a medium-sized kiln for brick making. How to get rich with limited land and resources became a tough question haunting Wang Hongbin, the then newly appointed party secretary.

Wang started by building a wheat flour mill. Wheat is the staple crop of the Central Plain where Henan province is located; however, there was not a single large wheat-milling plant in the area at that time. The idea was supported by other members in the Party Committee. Using the money borrowed by the Party Committee members from their relatives and friends and negotiating with the construction team for a credit on the payment, the Central Plain Flour Mill, with a daily output of 20 tons, was established in 1979.

Then, in 1980, Wang thought about the small mound in the village, which could be leveled and the earth used to produce bricks. Because many families had started to build new houses, bricks were in great demand. However, the challenge was where to get the money to start up the brickworks. Wang played a trick. He first held a meeting among cadres, spreading the news that to reward their hard work, each cadre's family could preorder 30,000 bricks (just enough to build a house) for at least 20 percent below market price, which meant that they could save a significant sum of money in material costs for building a house. The news quickly spread to Nanjie villagers and even neighboring villagers. Seeing that the bricks were so popular, people flocked to the Party Committee, requesting orders to buy the bricks in advance. Thus, the Party announced to the production teams that the sale of bricks was open to the public for three days, and each family was limited to an order of 30,000 bricks. Soon more than 13 million bricks were presold to the villagers, and more than 300,000 yuan (about US$43,000 using the 2010 exchange rate)[17] was collected. In August 1981, the brickworks began its commercial operation.[18] Here Wang made use of the villagers' assumption of cadre privileges to get initial capital for the collective enterprise.

In just over a year, Nanjie had established its two foundational village enterprises, and the industrial output reached 400,000 yuan – a breakthrough in Nanjie's industrial history. As a result, people often joked that Nanjie's prosperity started with "playing with clay eggs" (*wan nidan*, referring to brick making) and accelerated by "playing with bags of flour" (*wan miandan*, referring to flour manufacturing). However, since then the household responsibility system has dominated China, and contracting out suddenly became the panacea and standard practice in reform. Wang, quick to follow the national policy, approved the transfer of the two village enterprises to two "capable persons" in the village, and the brickworks was contracted out to Yu Yanlin in 1982. Nevertheless, privatized operations did not bring about economic prosperity. Although a few people in the village became wealthier than before, for most of the villagers, life had not improved. The contractors did not pay the workers or the village's contracting fee on

---

[17] The exchange rate in 1980 was artificially set at 1.50 to the dollar, not reflecting purchasing power parities. At the time, foreign trade played a very small part in China's economy. As a result, unless otherwise stated the 2010 dollar-yuan exchange rate is used in this book to give readers a rough idea of the quantity of money, but it is not adjusted for inflation.

[18] Since its operation, it provided the village with its initial capital as well as the bricks for houses and office buildings in the 1990s. The brickworks was closed down in September 1999, after all the major construction was complete.

time and squandered money on themselves. The balance sheet was a mess. Indignant villagers posted "big-character posters" (*dazibao*)[19] to the county government and even on Wang Hongbin's door.

Instead of blaming the contractors, people criticized the Village Party Committee for contracting out the enterprises, wondering if the Party Committee or Wang took any bribes from the contractors. In 1984, in light of the violation of the terms of the contracts by the contractors and despite the pressure from them and the larger trend of de-collectivization at the national level, Wang and the Party Committee decided to revoke the contract and took over the operation of the two enterprises. Wang volunteered to be the managing director of the two plants to clean up the mess. The output of the two plants doubled in the same year. Thus, the recentralization of resources in Nanjie was not a result of coercion or abuse of power, and it did not lead to people's protests and petitions as in many other rural areas. Instead, it was a way of preventing personal profiteering and exploring ways to improve the villagers' well-being.

At that time there were still other private enterprises in the village. In fact, villagers were encouraged to have their own businesses in the immediate years after 1978 when the reform and opening-up policy was adopted. However, entering the 1990s, private businesses disappeared in Nanjie. It was partly because of peer pressure, as most of the villagers joined the collective enterprises, and those "outliers" felt awkward and even ashamed working on their own, as a village is such a closely knit community. Because land has been re-collectivized, private enterprises were actually occupying collective land. In addition, as collective enterprises became stronger, it was hard for private enterprises to compete, as most of the private enterprises were small and in the same industries as the collective enterprises. Furthermore, Nanjie started its social welfare system from the 1980s, and all the villagers, including those who were self-employed, enjoyed free water, electricity, and other services. The village would also pay agricultural taxes for them. As a result, even though the village did not ban the private economy at first, a combination of shame, peer pressure, and/or concern about profits drove villagers to either sell their businesses to the collective or simply close them down and join the collective enterprises.

Once the village had taken back the operation of the two plants, expanding sales became the most severe challenge. In 1984, to explore market opportunities, Wang Hongbin and the vice party secretary Wang Jinzhong

---

[19] *Dazibao* were widely used during the Cultural Revolution as a way of expressing criticism of and dissatisfaction with a particular activity or a specific person.

took a bus to carry the flour Nanjie produced to the capital, Beijing. Through their contact with a Nanjier who worked in Beijing, they visited a large food-manufacturing plant – the Beijing Jingsong Pastry Factory – to promote Nanjie flour and received a 15-year supply contract.[20] The same year Nanjie built a branch factory of this business and soon started to manufacture pastries, including mooncakes, rice crusts, biscuits, and dried noodles. The construction was completed in May 1985, and that factory was the predecessor of the Nanjie Instant Noodle Factory that has made the village famous in China and around the world.

In 1989, Nanjie bought its first production line of instant noodles from Jingsong Pastry and started to produce Yingsong instant noodles, which later became a brand whose quality received an award from the state. This was also the first instant noodle factory in Henan province, despite Henan's huge production of wheat. Along with other pastries, Nanjie developed its food-processing industry as the core of its industrial strategy. Meanwhile, Nanjie opened a second flour mill in 1991 to satisfy the increasing demand from the instant noodles factory. The same year Nanjie Village became the wealthiest village in Henan manufacturing more than 100 million yuan (roughly US$20 million based on the 1991 exchange rate) of output, more than 300 times the figure of a decade before. Entering the 1990s, Nanjie opened several joint ventures,[21] including a color printing factory (using Japanese equipment); an offset printing factory (employing German machines)[22]; the Nande Food Company and the Maien Food Company,[23] which are joint ventures with

---

[20] Nanjie's archived documents, volume 5.

[21] The foreign partners in these joint ventures do not participate in the daily management of the enterprises but only provide capital and/or equipment and receive their share of the profits. Maien and the color printing factory used to be managed by the Japanese representative Zhou Jinghua. However, in 1996 Nanjie renegotiated a contract with the Japanese investor and took over both businesses' daily operations. Wang Hongbin said that Nanjie and Zhou Jinghua disagreed on their management strategies and that Nanjie should not politically succumb to the Japanese partner, even though that meant giving up certain economic interests (Nanjie Archived Documents, Vol. 50). Clearly Wang Hongbin wanted to make sure that joint ventures would not affect the basic political and social institutions in the Nanjie community.

[22] Printing factories originally printed packages for the instant noodles factories and later became an industry of their own and accepted orders from outside the village.

[23] Nande Food Company produces various kinds of ramen noodles, including those that are microwavable, and I found its products with the brand Nanjiecun (Nanjie Village) sold at a major Chinese supermarket, Super 88, in South Boston in the United States in 2005. Nanjie also has an instant noodles factory, which is totally self-financed and owned. The Maien Food Company mainly produces snacks such as chocolate-covered biscuit sticks, which are very popular in East Asia. Each year, a large number of its products are exported to a Chocolate Sticks Festival in Korea.

Japan; and the Nande Beer Factory,[24] which is a joint venture with Hong Kong. Based on instant noodles and branching out into ancillary industries such as spices, printing, and packaging, Nanjie thus developed into a large corporate group covering various industries, some of which are export oriented.

## Social Welfare: Building a Socialist Heaven

Nanjie villagers have enjoyed a free supply of water since 1982 and a free power supply since 1986. In 1989, the Linying County Utility Bureau built a substation to meet Nanjie Village's civil and industrial power needs.

The comprehensive social welfare system, however, started in 1991, when the village's total output exceeded 100 million yuan. According to the size of the household, each family was provided with free coal briquettes for cooking and heating. The village also distributed meat to its members during the Spring Festival, Lantern Festival, Mid-Autumn Festival, and New Year – pork for Han and beef for Hui people.

Because of the scarce land, the Party Committee proposed the development of high-rise buildings. From 1992 to 1997, villagers gradually moved out of their original houses and took up residence in furnished apartment buildings (Figure 2.2). Depending on the size of the household, villagers moved into either two-bedroom or three-bedroom apartments; households of more than five people and three generations were assigned with two or three suites of two-bedroom apartments. Villagers of different ethnicities, village teams, and genealogies were mixed in residence, with younger people being assigned to upper floors and older people lower floors. Each apartment is provided with the same furniture, electrical appliances, and free central air-conditioning and heating. Since then, coal briquettes have been replaced by gas. Now the distribution of free supplies is on a monthly basis, and the items have been expanded from meat to almost everything needed in people's daily lives – from everyday necessities such as vegetables, spices, drinks, cooking oil, and snacks[25] to major services such as funeral and wedding expenses, housing, travel, education (including subsidies of students' living expenses and free meal plans), and medical care. Converting the welfare into cash, since 2000, each villager, including children, has on average

---

[24] The equipment in the factory was imported from Germany, which according to Mr. Li Weimin, director of Nanjie's International Department, is the same as that used in the famous Chinese brand Tsingtao Beer.

[25] Since 2006, villagers have been provided with welfare coupons that can be exchanged for the same value of items they want at the village supermarkets to better cater to individual tastes.

Figure 2.2.  Apartment buildings in Nanjie.

enjoyed about 6,000 yuan of welfare annually in addition to their salaries.[26]
As a comparison, the average total income per capita for rural residents
in the central part of China, where Henan province is located, has been
around 3,000 yuan.[27]

To this day, Nanjie Village is perhaps most attractive to the old and the
young. It encourages all the elderly people who can no longer work to go
to the nursing home built and sustained by the village. There the elderly
are taken care of and provided with free food, housing, entertainment, and
medical care. This is a huge change in mentality from the tradition that
the elderly should be cared for by their children, and unless they have no
children, living in a nursing home is highly stigmatized, especially in rural

---

[26] According to an internal document on the medical and welfare expenses enjoyed by the
villagers, in 2000, on average, each villager was provided with welfare worth of 5,987 yuan;
in 2001, 6,079 yuan; in 2002, 6,282 yuan; and in 2003, 6,262 yuan.

[27] Statistics from the Chinese Agricultural Development Report on the Web site of the
Ministry of Agriculture (http://www.agri.gov.cn/sjzl/baipshu.htm) indicate that the average total income per capita was 2,893 yuan in 2000, 3,116 yuan in 2001, 3,259 yuan in
2002, and 3,350 yuan in 2003 in the central part of China. Regional data in the report are
categorized into the eastern, central, and western parts.

China. This is also partly why, to have more security in their later years, parents prefer sons rather than daughters. Such a preference seems irrelevant in Nanjie, at least not out of economic concerns. In the nursing home, elderly people enjoy their own lives and become good company for each other. Zang Ai, who has been a Party member for almost sixty years, was very proud of the achievements made by Nanjie. She said she could not stop smiling even when having meals (*chifan douzai xiao*). Another four elderly people were happily playing Mahjong when I was there. There is also a free public health clinic for the villagers. If the illness gets too serious, patients will be referred to larger hospitals and all the expenses will be reimbursed. Several elderly villagers were sent to hospitals in Zhengzhou, the capital city of Henan province, or Beijing for treatment of cancer and other diseases that many rural families could not afford.

For children, Nanjie's kindergarten, elementary school, and secondary school are equipped with state-of-the-art facilities and experienced teachers; some children living in Linying county also go to Nanjie for school. The village not only pays for tuition from kindergarten to college, but also provides students with subsidies of living expenses and covers students' round tickets home during vacations. For college students who study in Henan province, each is given 250 yuan per month for personal expenses, and those who study outside the province are given 300 yuan per month.[28] The elderly people were proud to tell me that among Nanjie's younger generations, 15 went to graduate school, one got a PhD degree, and 377 people received education equal to, or above, the secondary school level. For those who cannot get admitted to college, the village will send them to vocational schools and pay the expenses. Students, however, are not required to go back to Nanjie to work after graduation.

Having provided a brief account of the village's history of land ownership, economic structure, and social welfare, over the past fifty years, I will now turn to the current situation in Nanjie.

## The Village at First Glance

### Slogans and Chairman Mao
Nanjie is proud of its rapid economic growth as well as its adherence to the communist ideology. When driving from Linying county to Nanjie Village,

---

[28] According to my latest interview with the director of the Corporate Management Office, Mr. Zhang, in 2010, the village pays each college student who studies in Henan 300 yuan and others 400 yuan per month.

Figure 2.3.  Mao's statue.

you will find that the roads and facilities in Nanjie are tidier and wider than those in the county. The main road, Chaoyang (Sun-facing) Avenue, broad and spotless, leads to the Red East Square (*Dongfanghong Guangchang*), where a 9-meter-high, white-marble, statue of Mao is located, flanked by the portraits of Marx, Engels, Lenin, and Stalin (Figure 2.3). The statue was built for the centennial celebration of Mao's birth in 1993. The armed Village Militia members guard the statue 24 hours a day. Inscribed on the pedestal of the statue are words saying that "Mao Zedong is a human being, not God, but Mao Zedong Thought is greater than God."

A Tiananmen-Square-like construction, Chaoyang Gate, is located at the other end of Chaoyang Avenue, separating Nanjie from its neighboring village, Beijie (North Street) Village. Inside the village near the residential district, there is a long enclosed corridor, the Culture Corridor (*Wenhua Changlang*), built in 1997. Walking in the corridor, children going to school will not get wet or sunburned. The Culture Corridor is literally a museum of Chinese Communist Party (CCP) history, with pictures and excerpts from Party leaders' works. With the revolutionary songs of the Maoist era, such as "Sailing the Sea Depends on the Helmsman" (*dahai hangxing kao duoshou*) and "The East is Red" (*dongfanghong*), piped out of the public speakers in the village, one gets the illusion of being back in the old times. It is a contradiction of time: on the one hand, time seems to be frozen in that moment of history that has almost faded out of people's memory; on the other hand, the theme-park-like roads, high-rises, factories, and tourist attractions remind visitors of the hyperreality of modernity.

There are two book stores, three grocery stores, several restaurants and canteens, gift shops, a branch of the Chinalife Insurance Company, and the China Agriculture Bank,[29] as well as many other facilities in the village. All are quite new. Once you walk into the village, you will find two things that are most impressive. One is that no matter whether you are in the shops, in the offices, or at villagers' homes, there is always a statue of Chairman Mao placed in a salient position. The commodities that the gift shop and book stores sell are mostly related to Chairman Mao, including statues, pins, and copies of Mao's works. The other is that there are slogans hanging or painted on the walls everywhere of mostly instructive, encouraging, and philosophically meaningful maxims (Figure 2.4). For example, in the residential districts, many maxims praising collectivism are painted on the exterior walls of the apartment buildings, such as "a drop of water will turn into vapor unless it joins the sea, a person will gain full strength when he adjusts his personal pursuits to those of the collective."

Mr. Sheng, director of the Nanjie Newspaper Agency, told me that many of the slogans were created by the young intellectuals in the village or taken from well-known works by Mao, Marx, Lenin, and writers such as Lu Xun.[30] It seems that Nanjie has attracted some intelligent young people and individuals with the same ideals from other places. Those people, although not Nanjie villagers by origin, are awarded the status of "honorary villagers," and except for not having a Nanjie *hukou*, they enjoy the same benefits as the rest of the community. The former deputy director of the Nanjie Archives, Zhang Tianshun, was one of the honorary villagers, who left the village on my third visit there in 2006. He learned about Nanjie Village from the media and came to join the village in 1997 from Gansu, a province in northwestern China. He was a retired worker from a steel factory.

Lü Xiaohu is also an honorary villager. He joined Nanjie after his graduation from the Physical Education Department at Xinyang Normal Institute

---

[29] To have a bank branch in a village indicates the special economic position of Nanjie.

[30] Lu Xun is a patriotic Chinese writer famous for his acrimonious essays and novels, criticizing dogmatic Confucianism, the corrupt old Chinese society, and the weaknesses of the Chinese. He is often regarded as one of the key figures in the New Literature Movement in contemporary China, writing in plain Chinese about ordinary people with a political purpose.

Figure 2.4.   Slogans on the exterior walls of buildings.

and has been in Nanjie since 1994. His wife, who originally worked for the county's machinery factory, joined the village sales sector after her original factory closed down. There were 918 honorary villagers as of 2004, and they are clearly the intellectual and managerial backbone of the village.

The day I first arrived in Nanjie, December 26, 2003, was coincidentally the 110th birthday of Chairman Mao. All the villagers gathered in the Red East Square in front of Mao's statue. After Wang Hongbin's speech, an actor representing Chairman Mao appeared and spoke to the villagers in a Hunan accent. Villagers, who were originally scattered and silent, suddenly walked or ran toward "Chairman Mao" and gathered around him. Some elderly people were apparently very excited, and young people asked "Chairman Mao" for signatures. In a time when people usually chase after pop stars, Mao Zedong is an idol to many villagers.

In the summer of 2004, when I visited Nanjie for the second time, Lü Xiaohu gave me a pocket-size *Red Bible*. It includes a list of 100 questions that people may encounter in everyday life, such as "what to do when being scolded" and "what to do if my suggestion is not accepted by my boss." You can find the answers to those everyday problems by turning to the page with corresponding quotations from Mao. Of course, the quotes do not always answer the questions well, but their efforts to demonstrate that Maoism is not dead but can be rather pragmatic are rather impressive. The village also started the so-called red tourism (*hongse lüyou*), attracting people from all over China to visit this communist village as a way to increase revenue as well as gain recognition. Everyday touring carts carry visitors to the village's exhibition hall, dining hall, shops, factories, apartment buildings, botanical garden, the replica of Chairman Mao's childhood residence in Hunan, and the replicas of the Yan'an Pagoda and other important sites in the CCP's revolutionary history. In 2005 alone, Nanjie received 400,000 visits. In fact, Linying county moved its tourist company to Nanjie Village, given that Nanjie is probably the most important tourist attraction in the area.

Using a past ideology and political leader as the tool for holding people together and educating them is the first distinctive feature of Nanjie Village. It not only legitimizes the village's insistence on collective ownership and the pursuit of communal living, but also differentiates Nanjie from other villages. Furthermore, it serves two other functions: it is an effective way of attracting people from other areas who are not satisfied with the status quo, as well as serving as a method for getting economic and political resources from those upper-level governments that share similar ideals.

### The Search for Equality

The relative equality of all villagers is another distinctive feature of Nanjie Village. Because of the high welfare benefits, villagers are guaranteed decent housing, education, and health care. This mitigates the conflict between local government and villagers, because their income and benefits are almost the same. One of the most serious problems concerning Chinese peasants is that they have to face double inequality – that is, the relative poverty compared to urbanites and the relative poverty with respect to some local cadres and/or entrepreneurs. In Nanjie, however, as the major means of livelihood are also collectively owned and provided, economic inequality is not as controversial. Of course, there are other kinds of inequality that we will consider later.

Each villager gets about the same welfare distribution, living in apartments of almost the same size with similar pieces of furniture. Villagers are guaranteed jobs in village enterprises. Even though the nature of their work may vary, they receive about the same salaries – 250 yuan or so a month. There is a well-known slogan hung in a salient position in the village, saying "this world is for fools; it is supported and created by fools, and will eventually belong to fools" (*zhege shijie shi shazi de shijie, you shazi qu zhichi, you shazi qu zhuangzao, zuihou shi shuyu shazide*). Here "fools" obviously means those who can sacrifice their personal interests for the pursuit of equality and collective prosperity, and getting a salary as little as 250 yuan a month in such a rich village is also part of being a fool, given that 250 is a way of calling people foolish in many Chinese dialects.

## Behind the Scene

### A Two-Tiered System

I have always been fascinated by the similarities between different social systems. From Ancient Greece to the contemporary United States and China, many societies are two-tiered – a group of people's privileges are built upon the exploitation of another group(s) of people, or the comfort of the few is dependent on the poverty of the many. In Ancient Greece, this was achieved by slavery, in the United States through citizenship, and in China via the rural-urban division. Even in a community as small as Nanjie Village, the seemingly equal distribution is based on a two-tiered system.

Not all the people in Nanjie receive the same social welfare benefits. Those who are not Nanjie residents, but simply work in the factories or schools in Nanjie, get fewer social benefits yet receive a better salary than the villagers. Nanjie calls its distribution system "high social welfare benefits and low salaries for villagers, and low social welfare benefits and high salaries for non-villagers." It justifies its two-level distribution system by claiming that the reason migrant workers come to Nanjie is to earn money, thus salaries are more important than welfare benefits. Nanjie only has slightly more than 3,000 residents, around half of who are working in the village enterprises, but there are about 8,000 workers from other villages (Table 2.1).[31] That is to say, the majority of the workers in the enterprises are not Nanjie villagers, and this section of the labor force does not enjoy the benefits that Nanjie is proud of, except for free meals and accommodation and the occasional distribution of some fruits and Nanjie Village products.

The villagers call those migrant workers "workers from the outside" (*waigong*), in contrast to "workers from the inside" (*neigong*), referring to the villagers who work in the factories. Moreover, I was told in the

---

[31] According to my interview with Mr. Zhang, as of 2010, the number of migrant workers was around 7,000, fewer than that in 1997 when the village had almost 12,000 migrant workers, the largest number in its history. He said that the reduced number of workers was because of two reasons: first, the village factories had shed excess workers to raise efficiency; second, the salaries offered by Nanjie were not as attractive as many other enterprises, and there were also more businesses in the region competing for labor.

Table 2.1. *Numbers of workers in Nanjie, 1999–2004*

|  | 1999 | 2000 | 2001 | 2002 | 2003 | 2004 |
|---|---|---|---|---|---|---|
| Male | 3910 | 3820 | 3890 | 4451 | 3790 | 3581 |
| Female | 5879 | 5862 | 5546 | 6107 | 5755 | 6047 |
| Villagers | 1551 | 1650 | 1750 | 1980 | 2051 | 2051 |
| Non-villagers | 8238 | 8032 | 7686 | 8578 | 7494 | 7577 |
| Party members | 336 | 360 | 384 | 409 | 434 | 458 |
| Youth League members | 893 | 1078 | 1468 | 1888 | 2348 | 2400 |
| Age 18–23 | 5759 | 5717 | 5628 | 7109 | 5982 | 6382 |
| Age 24–35 | 3070 | 3047 | 2972 | 2389 | 2403 | 2266 |
| Age 36 above | 960 | 918 | 836 | 1060 | 1160 | 980 |

*Source*: Data are provided by the Village Labor Resource Office. Year 2004 is from January to July.

interviews with the migrant workers in 2006 that their monthly salaries a few years back were less than 100 yuan (about US$14), and some could get 100 to 200 yuan, which was not at all higher than the villagers as the officials claimed. At the time of the interviews, they were paid on average 500 to 600 yuan, and some could get up to 800 yuan – usually the more skilled workers and those who had stayed longer. When talking about salaries, they were very excited about the increasing income, offering no complaints, so I infer that the numbers they provided are true, not deliberately understated. The figures were confirmed in my interview with a Hui villager, Erwei, who opened his own restaurant outside the Chaoyang Gate. Erwei explained that the village had no choice but to raise the salaries for migrant workers in recent years; otherwise, nobody would want to work in Nanjie. Of course, engineers, managing specialists, and other highly qualified professionals are paid according to market prices. Some are paid more than 300,000 yuan (roughly US$43,000) a year.

In this sense, Nanjie is similar to the cities that have assimilated a certain amount of surplus rural labor but have not solved the problem of getting the labor integrated into their social system. This may eventually be threatening and detrimental to the system itself. It also shows the limited influence of Nanjie. Within a small village, it may be easy to safeguard the high level of social welfare and social equality, but how applicable is this pattern to other regions or larger areas?

Nonetheless, it is noticeable that migrant workers in Nanjie are treated better than in many other places. That is also why people from outside the village still choose to work there. They do not need to work overtime with high intensity or in health-threatening conditions such as workers in the sweatshops. Their rooms are supplied with free air-conditioning and heating, although they live in a much smaller space than the villagers: eight people sharing a dorm room with steel-framed bunk beds. There is a TV room and a public bathroom on each floor. They also receive a gradually increasing level of medical benefits for each year of employment. Those who have worked in the village for five years and have received at least one award for excellence at work will enjoy the same medical benefits as villagers. According to the migrant workers I interviewed, the medical benefits are directly added to their salaries. In addition, migrant workers usually sign a three-year contract with Nanjie. They have four days off each month plus legal holidays. It is also possible to ask for personal leaves. Xiao Xue, for example, went back home for a while to get married, and returned afterward to continue her contract. Most of the migrant workers are females between 18 and 23 years old, fresh out of school, so security is also an issue that they consider when choosing their job location. Nanjie is seen to be safer and simpler than other places; there is hardly any crime in the village – no gambling, pickpocketing, robberies, or prostitution – and people, including supervisors, are easy to get along with. All these factors seem to concern the majority of the migrant workers in the village more than monetary gains.

Unless one has a special talent needed in the village, such as an experienced manager, a skilled teacher, or a person with strong networks, there are mainly two ways for a migrant worker to achieve upward mobility: one is by becoming an honorary villager, and the other one is by marrying a villager.

In 2003, the Party Committee issued an official document on how to recruit and manage honorary villagers.[32] In the document, it stipulates that only couples who both work in Nanjie, with one working for more than ten years and receiving more than five awards and the other working for more than six years and receiving in excess of three awards, are eligible to apply for the honorary villager status. If, however, the person possesses talent, a good education, and special skills, he or she can apply after working in Nanjie for three years, subject to the Party Committee's approval. Moreover, since 2003, those who have already become honorary villagers have to be awarded for their excellence at work at least once every three years; otherwise, their honorary villager status will be revoked. In addition, only one child of the honorary villager family can inherit the status, which may be an effective way to enforce the state's one-child policy. The honorary

---

[32] The document is titled "Regulations on Workers' Welfare, Recruiting Honorary Villagers, and Enhancing the Management of Honorary Villagers." It was the No. 1 document in 2003.

villager status will be canceled for girls after their marriages, and for boys, the status cannot be inherited by their wives or children. It is interesting to notice that the gender difference in the regulations reflects China's virilocal tradition.[33] However, according to some of the interviewees, almost no honorary villager status has been granted in recent years as a result of the economic slowdown.

During the interviews, I also met many people who have become villagers through marriages. They are called Nanjie's "sons-in-law" (*Nanjie de nüxu*) or "daughters-in-law" (*Nanjie de xifu*). Xiaorui, who came to Nanjie in 1993, is one of Nanjie's daughters-in-law. She told me that she was originally employed at the Village Transportation Team and had to start work at seven in the morning. Life then was fast paced and hectic. She now works in the Labor Resource Office, a change from a blue-collar job to a white-collar job. She said that the majority of the villagers work in the back offices as administrators, and some who have technical skills also work in the enterprises. A few who do not have any special talents will have to take manual jobs in the workshops. According to Xiaorui, Nanjie is quite strict in screening its future daughters-in-law. The village will send people to the girl's hometown to do a background check. If the girl has a bad record locally, the village will suggest that the boy should not marry her. Each year a collective wedding will be held for new couples in the village, usually during the New Year celebration, and they will be sent on a honeymoon to Yan'an, the old revolutionary base for the CCP, or to Beijing. No individual weddings are allowed to prevent people from excessive dining, drinking, gift giving, and money squandering, which are considered to be "uncivilized" ritualistic activities.

Such a two-tiered system does not stop at the villager–migrant-worker division, but extends to differences among the villagers. First of all, not all villagers get 250 yuan a month; 250 is, in fact, the ceiling salary. Depending on the nature of the job, villagers can get as low as 80 yuan a month, such as those who do cleaning. Mr. Duan, director of the Party Committee Administration Office, said that salaries range from 150 to 250 yuan, a very small difference, according to him. However, this is different from what I learned on my first visit to the village, when almost everyone told me that all villagers were paid the same, 250 yuan. In 2006, Xiao Li, who was then a college student who returned to Nanjie for the winter break, told me that

---

[33] In China, traditionally, marriages are virilocal. Daughters, once married, are expected to live with their husbands' families, sharing the chores, and of course, also enjoying the family benefits. Their responsibilities and welfare in their parents' families cease after their marriages.

his parents worked as salespeople in the village, and they were paid far more than 250 yuan, and could get commissions for each deal they made. Also, some cadres are allowed to sign the bills for dining at the village restaurants and accommodation at the Village Hotel to the collective account, enabling them to receive guests from the outside. A professor who used to do research on Nanjie informed me that Zhang Tianshun, vice director of the archives, complained that the village leaders failed to pay him enough respect, and their refusal to grant him the right to sign the bills was one of his concerns. Erwei also mentioned:

There is a vehicle team in the village. That is for cadres! If an ordinary villager calls for a ride, who will care? See, I have my own car, and I can go wherever I want to go. Now a lot of cadres try every means to turn public property into their own property, and put collective money into their own pockets. The salaries paid by the village are too little. Many villagers are secretly running their own businesses, but dare not disclose it to the village. They are afraid that their jobs, welfare benefits, and income in the village will be deducted or eliminated. I'm not afraid, though. I work for myself now.

It seems that in addition to the rationed social welfare benefits, there is also a "grey" area of income for villagers, and that part varies with regard to one's power, mores, and the nature of the job.

In addition, honorary villagers can be treated very differently, based on their contribution to the village and their own initiative including networking abilities. Some of the honorary villagers get exactly the same benefits, if not more, as the villagers. Some, however, still live in the old "affiliates' building" (*jiashu lou*), with only one room for each family and shared bathrooms.

### Monolith or Mosaic?

There is a famous saying by Wang Hongbin: "happiness is not the same as being rich, but being rich is part of happiness" (*fuyu budengyu xingfu, xingfu baokuo fuyu*). Walking around the village, you will see people exercising or chatting in front of their apartment buildings, and if you talk to them, nine times out of ten, you will hear them say how happy their lives are, or in their local dialect, *kexingfu*, meaning "very happy, very lucky." If you talk to the migrant workers or people from neighboring villages, they will most likely display their jealousy of Nanjiers and tell you that Nanjie people are so lucky (*kexingfu*).

What exactly does happiness mean for Nanjie villagers? Is it the prosperity of the collective? Is being "a fool" part of this happiness? Or is it simply the welfare benefits they are enjoying, which not many other villages can provide? Are they happy because they are the altruistic few that take the pursuit of equality seriously or because they are merely the rational *homo economicus* trying to maximize their own utility? I asked almost every one of my interviewees to define happiness, but none of them seemed to be able to give me a definite answer. I started to wonder if the communist ideology has really taken root in people's mind and become the driving force and common goal of people. If not, to what extent is collectivism, or the ideology of sacrificing oneself for the benefits of the whole, effective in the management of the village?

Then I asked people what they think of Mao Zedong and his thoughts. The older generation, mostly people in their fifties and sixties, usually could not help quoting words from Mao's works and speeches. Mr. Duan, for example, said, citing Mao, that communism must rely on the ultimate enhancement of two aspects of society: people's morality and material production. He also quoted Mao on how to solve the problems facing rural China, saying that the key is to level the gaps between the urban and rural areas, between workers and peasants, and between manual workers and mental workers, and that Nanjie is right on this track. Mr. Wang, director of the archives, commented:

Mao Zedong Thought is not timeless, but the essence of his thoughts is eternal, for example, his works on anti-liberalism and on serving the people. It [Mao Zedong Thought] provides the spiritual support, similar to the functions of religions, such as Buddhism, Taoism, and Christianity. There needs to be a thought, a belief, to unite people. In today's China, Confucianism won't do, for it is from feudal China and is already out-dated. Deng Xiaoping's theories are more on the economy, less on morality. So it has to be Mao Zedong Thought! After all, people are very familiar with Mao's works, and have special feelings towards them. To follow Marxism, Leninism, and Mao Zedong Thought is also the policy of the central government!

People in their thirties or early forties would agree on the importance of Mao Zedong's thoughts but obviously do not know as much as the more senior people. Xiaorui, for example, said that Mao's thoughts are part of Nanjie's corporate culture and that the villagers adore Chairman Mao, but she did not know why the village chose Mao's thoughts as their guidelines in the first place. All she felt was that Mao is more influential in China than Deng Xiaoping, and Deng Xiaoping's theories are based on Mao's.

The younger generations seem to only care about the relatively good living conditions Nanjie provides. Taking a break from his computer game and online chatting,[34] Xiao Li, who was studying at a printing institute in

---

[34] In Nanjie, each apartment is provided with Internet access and so are most of the offices. There are also Internet cafes in the nearby county center. Besides, the village has its own TV station and provides villagers with more than forty channels.

Beijing, told me that he found that the living standard in Nanjie is much higher than many other places. While he was at school, he always thought that life at home was better and happier. Obviously, here happiness means material comfort rather than self-sacrifice or collective prosperity.

The generation gap can also be seen in the different attitudes toward a collective economy. Erwei's father, for example, was very positive about Nanjie's current path.[35] He said that his life is happy and safe. Every month he gets flour, cooking oil, and other necessities and does not have to worry about a lack of food or shelter. "If I were in other villages," he said, "who would care about you? Nobody would care about you, even if you stayed in bed for three days." According to him, Nanjie, unlike other villages, is not satisfied with a few wealthy people; instead, it is pursuing the goal of everyone being wealthy together. Although as individuals, some people may earn less than they can, as a collective, they are rich.

His son, however, belongs to those "some people." He obviously is dissatisfied with getting the same income as those who cannot work or do not have any talent. Therefore, he chose to leave the collective and explore his own path. Nevertheless, he still lives in the villagers' building inside Nanjie and enjoys free electricity, water, air-conditioning, and heat, although other welfare benefits are no longer provided to him. This also indicates the increasing tolerance of the Village Party Committee toward dissidents. Erwei, on the other hand, also expressed his willingness to rejoin the collective, if he was given a position in the village leadership, and he still wanted the collective to be successful.

### Nanjie's "Resident Aliens"

Honorary villagers are a very special group of people in Nanjie. They came from different places of origin and various backgrounds and chose to settle down in a village, although their *hukou* belongs elsewhere. They usually work as administrators, occupying more white-collar jobs than many other migrant workers and enjoying the welfare benefits only meant for villagers. Still they are not villagers, as they do not have Nanjie residency and

[35] It was a coincidence that I interviewed both the father and the son. I interviewed Erwei's father first. The next day, I walked out of the Chaoyang Gate, in hope of learning about the opinions of people from the neighboring villages about Nanjie, and randomly chose a couple, who are Beijie villagers. While we were talking, a young man in his thirties joined us. The couple told me that he was a Nanjie villager but was now self-employed (*dan'gan*). This interested me a lot, so I talked in depth with him. Toward the end of the conversation, I asked if he would mind telling me his name, and he told me his name. I said I just interviewed another man with the same last name. Then I discovered that it was, in fact, his father.

thus cannot vote or be promoted to top positions in the leadership, yet they are free to leave the village if they want. They have the talents that Nanjie needs, but there is clearly a glass ceiling in their career path. So why did they choose Nanjie and choose to remain there, given that many have been in the village for more than a decade?

Qü Yuhong, a woman in her thirties, worked at the Village Women's Federation Office in 2006 in charge of family planning, divorce coordination, and other women-related issues.[36] She is from Luoyang, located in the western part of Henan province, and was recruited to Nanjie fresh out of college with a number of her schoolmates in 1995. This was when Nanjie's Ramen Noodle Factory imported a new production line from Japan and was in need of well-educated workers. Her major was corporate management, but during her years in Nanjie, she mainly worked as the secretary of the Youth League subbranch, first at the Noodle Factory and then the flour mill. She was also employed as a statistician for some time and was transferred to her current office in August 2001. Her husband is also an honorary villager and was in charge of sales at the flour mill at the time.

Several people in her cohort have already left Nanjie. "They couldn't get used to the life here. Some were dissatisfied with the salary, and you know, it is sometimes difficult for young people to get used to the environment here. Some are doing pretty well now." When I asked why she chose to stay, she smiled and answered:

I like the environment here. It's a good environment for work and living. Plus I am not a very extrovert person, not very ambitious, either. I'm from the rural area, and my family can't provide me with a better job. I have settled down here, and if I leave, what about my husband and son? My son goes to school in Nanjie, and the quality of education there is pretty good. They start to teach English in kindergarten. I'm now learning with my son, picking up my English and also tutoring him. I think it'll be easy for him to find a job in the future, if he can learn English well. That's what the larger environment requires. Nanjiers are guileless and genuine (*pushi*), and they care about your work and study. There are no complicated things like in other places [meaning cheating and internal politics among colleagues], and people are easy to get along with.

When I asked if she is ever jealous of her schoolmates who have left Nanjie and are doing well, she expressed satisfaction with her current life.

Having money doesn't mean that you are happy. The other day my boy was watching a cartoon, and commented, "Mom, isn't it good to have a lot of money? That way we can buy whatever we want." And I told him that his thought was wrong. You see

---

[36] I learned in 2011 that she was reappointed to Nanjie's Newspaper Agency.

that many self-employed people outside are very rich, but their living and working environment is not that good, and they don't necessarily feel happy. Actually their jobs can be very demanding and stressful, and some of them have to sacrifice their family or get divorced. I think I'm pretty happy now. I don't have much pressure, and I have a happy family.

She invited me to her home, and I got a chance to meet her son, a lovely boy who likes watching cartoons. Yuhong urged his son to speak English with me, and the little boy reluctantly moved his eyes from the cartoon he was watching and told me that he saw crocodiles, monkeys, and giraffes in the zoo the other day. I could see that her son was the focus of her life. Her apartment is smaller than the villagers', even though she is an honorary villager, but she showed me the rooms and the balcony with great pride. They have to share a public bathroom with other residents on the floor, whereas the villagers live in apartments with private bathrooms. She and her husband offered to treat me to a dinner at a nearby restaurant, but I politely turned down the invitation, thinking of their low cash income. Still I could feel her happiness. Maybe her home is nothing for a person who grows up in a big city and who is used to spacious and well-decorated apartments and maybe working as an administrator dealing with boring documents and reports and receiving a low income with little prospect of being promoted is the last choice for many college graduates, but it is what Yuhong chose, and she seems to be satisfied with her choice for now.

Zhu Chunjing, a man in his forties, is the office director of the currently most profitable factory in Nanjie, the Spices Factory. He used to work as a journalist in the Nanjie Newspaper Agency. He is very eloquent and talkative. His father and mother are both from Henan, but he was born in Zunyi in southwest China, where his father was performing his military duty. He barely has a Henan accent.

My father's generation didn't have much choice. They would go to wherever the state wanted them to go. In 1962 during the severe economic recession in China, people were encouraged to go back to their places of origin (*cong na er lai, hui na er qu*), so my mom went back to her hometown, Linying county [where Nanjie is located]. But there was no land or house left for her in Linying, so life was very difficult. My dad brought me back to Guiyang [capital of Guizhou] after my mom's death in 1970. In 1980, I was assigned a job in the Fourth Bureau of the China Construction Engineering Corporation led by the Ministry of Construction, because of my dad's affiliation, and stayed there till 1995. In 1982, I was sent by my work unit to help construct the coal mine in Anhui, and stayed there for 12 years, and then left for Guangdong [a rich coastal province in southern China, which took the lead in China's reform and opening-up era]. It was in Guangdong that I accidentally saw a newspaper story on Nanjie, and Nanjie was described as a very good place in the story. Because I went to Nanjie in 1989 to visit my aunt and cousins,

I knew what Nanjie was like, and I couldn't believe that Nanjie would change so much in six years. I thought that the story must have been exaggerated, so I called my younger cousin to find the truth. To my surprise, my cousin said that Nanjie had indeed developed a lot. So I was starting to think about quitting my job at China Construction and go to Nanjie. Although China Construction had better salaries and perks, my life was very unstable. My wife was in the same company, and we had to move from time to time for job relocation, and my son, who was then 3 years old, would be going to school soon. If we stayed in the same company, my son would have to transfer to different schools with us and live an unstable life, which is not good for his development. So I brought 1,000 yuan and came to Nanjie with my son in 1995 to see if it's worthwhile to begin a new life here, and if not, I would simply take it as a vacation to visit my relatives (*zou qinqi*). After arriving in Nanjie, I found that the salaries here were pretty low, and the Squad Leader (*banzhang*, meaning the Party Secretary Wang Hongbin) only had a monthly salary of 250 yuan, while I earned more than 1,000 yuan a month at that time. Because we worked in southern China, and had more contacts with people from Hong Kong, I knew that in Hong Kong, a truck driver could earn 8,000 to 9,000 yuan a month then, some could even earn 10,000 yuan.

However, for the sake of his son, he still chose Nanjie. His wife could not stand the low income and refused to go to Nanjie with him, so they divorced, and his son stayed with him for a more stable environment and more accessible education.

He is not yet an honorary villager, for as a single father, he is not qualified for such an application. During much of the time he has been in Nanjie, he lived in a converted office room at the Nanjie Newspaper Agency. He moved into a dormitory building for married migrant workers a year ago, where he met his current wife, a single mother with her son living next door. "We have a similar attitude toward life. We don't pay much attention to material comfort, but enjoy a simple, stable life." He felt happy biking around Nanjie with his son and treated him to a meal at a restaurant outside the Chaoyang Gate with his meager income. "People are very friendly here. I have also made friends with other migrants, like Director Sheng [of the Village Newspaper Agency] and Lü Xiaohu. Moreover, the Squad Leader is a very decent and kind-hearted man; he has a lot of charisma."

Gu Yi, a man with a master's degree from Beijing University of Aeronautics and Astronautics, joined Nanjie after his graduation in 2004. He is now the youngest one in the core leadership of Nanjie, head of the Maien Food Corporation, and vice managing director of the Nanjie Corporate Group. He is not from the region but was recommended to Wang Hongbin by one of his professors. He first visited Nanjie in the summer of 1997.

Because my family lives near the rural area, I know about peasants. At that time I heard about Nanjie, but I thought it was simply a village, and I didn't believe it would be anything special. However, once I was in Nanjie, I found that it was so different from other villages. My first impression was the infrastructure. I mean, the roads were just like cities. And I listened to the introduction, and learned that there were many factories in the village. For instant noodles alone, there were three factories! So I was very impressed by Nanjie on my first visit, an economically sound village. Salaries were not high, but life was stable and safe. Many parents in nearby villages wanted to send their children to work in Nanjie, because they thought their children wouldn't be corrupted in Nanjie (*xue bu huai*). I respected and admired the Squad Leader a lot. So in 1997 all I learned about Nanjie was positive. In 2004, Nanjie's economy began to slow down, and I also heard about some negative things. Of course, Nanjie was not the only one struck by the fiscal restraint of the state. I came to Nanjie mainly because the Squad Leader is respected, and I'm willing to work for him. Also, my major was navigation, but I don't want to be a technician; it can't contribute much to society. I want to learn about economics, and I think running a business is a good start, so I came here in August 2004 to get an overview of the corporation, and took over Maien in November.

Now his whole family, including his parents, lives in Nanjie. He has also been granted honorary villager status, getting 250 yuan a month, hardly a competitive salary for people with advanced degrees. However, he said he was prepared to do economic research on a low income or even without any pay before he joined Nanjie, so salary is not a priority for him.

I think different people have different pursuits. I remember once I was chatting with my friend. He said that he wishes that the luxury cars on the street were all his, and I joked, "Then I wish I could wave my hand and get a gang of people to destroy all those cars." One thing that I haven't recognized until recently is how simple the life of the local people is! Most people only have noodles with a little spinach or corn leaves for meals, and the consumption of meat, eggs, and dairy products is very low. They are used to that kind of life. One day my parents bought some meat, and the villagers they met on the way home asked which canteen they worked at. They thought the meat was for a canteen, not a household of four!

Obviously, Nanjie is not attractive to everyone. Although it is wealthier than many villages, the wage level is not as high as in the cities and villages of the coastal areas. For some people from the neighboring villages or other poor regions, its relatively better economic conditions and safer environment may be a reason to migrate to Nanjie. For others, in addition to the economic and safety incentives, there may be more reasons.

Yuhong, Chunjing, Yi, and many other Nanjie "resident aliens" are from very different backgrounds, but they seem to share something in common. They have a distinct philosophy of life, which is similar to Nanjie's *weltanschauung* – that is, being rich does not mean one is happy. In other words, they do not think that people's value can be measured by money alone, so they more or less agree with the distribution and incentive systems in

Nanjie and accept the life style there. Moreover, they respect the leaders in Nanjie, especially the Squad Leader, Wang Hongbin. In addition, they do not anticipate better opportunities in places other than Nanjie. As Chunjing said, "I'm already in my forties, and I don't think any other companies would hire me." They are more educated than the villagers but may not be so competitive in a national labor market. In the case of Yi, even though he has a master's degree, he is working in a completely different area from what he has learned at school. After all, how many graduates fresh out of school, without any experience and management expertise, can have a chance to run a multimillion dollar company?

### Circle on the Outside and Square on the Inside

"Circle on the outside, square on the inside" (*waiyuan neifang*) is the strategy officially promoted and implemented by Nanjie. It means that when doing business with the outside world, Nanjie will follow commercial practices and market rules. As Mr. Sheng put it, "necessary wining and dining will be provided, and necessary gifts will also be given (*gai qing de qing, gai song de song*)." Nanjie even built a separate luxury villa with mahjong tables and a Karaoke club for its foreign investors, although the villagers are not supposed to gamble or sing Karaoke. Inside the village, the importance of moral education and ethical progress is emphasized, featuring singing revolutionary songs, reciting the *Red Bible*, learning from Lei Feng – the role model of a comrade serving the people wholeheartedly – and so on. Gifts received are supposed to be handed over to the collective. This strategy itself indicates the powerlessness of Nanjie to change the larger context or the forces accompanying modernization, yet on the other hand, it seems to purposely separate Nanjie from the wider social and economic environment, dividing the world into Nanjie and the outside. As a result, when talking to the villagers, you can always hear people saying how their village is different from other places, or the outside (*waimian*), and how their villagers are more ethical.

Suffice it to say that the Nanjie model offers a possible path toward rural industrialization in a region lacking good natural resources, that is, to look for industries that can best exploit the local advantages, which, in the Nanjie case, is the food industry, given the large output of wheat and the supply of cheap labor in the area. With instant noodles as its core industry, Nanjie branched out into printing and spices, both of which were originally supporting facilities for instant noodles. The model also maintains the institutions that peasants are familiar with – the communal structure of the Maoist era. It makes use of the existing personnel, village leaders, who villagers know well, have good reputations, and can exert great influence on the members.

Nonetheless, how round can the circle be and how square is the square? When the circle meets the square, will the square be twisted to resemble the circle? Nanjie has its own rules and regulations in addition to the state laws to bind villagers.[37] Nanjie Village Code of Conduct (*Nanjiecun Cungui Minyue*) consists of three sections – morality, work, and life – and each section is divided into two parts: issues and settlements. For example, in the morality section, the sanction for "not willing to contribute to building the Nanjie community" is to revoke all the welfare benefits enjoyed by the whole family (parents, husband/wife, children), and the family cannot leave the community unless they repay the debt they owe to the village (the welfare benefits they have previously enjoyed). Their share of the land will be returned to them by the village's assignment.[38] For those having a second job outside the village, the punishment is to revoke all the welfare benefits.

To ensure that villagers follow the rules and devote themselves to the building of the Nanjie communist community, the village also creates a way to evaluate villagers' behavior, that is, through the "ten-star model family" contest (*shixingji wenminghu pingbi*) first started in 1992. Each star is associated with certain welfare benefits, so losing a star means paying for some of the previously free supplies. The ten stars are the stars of communism, responsibility, self-sacrifice, knowledge, obeying the law, following the new culture,[39] skills, thriftiness, kindness and filial obedience, and sanitation.[40] Evaluation forms are first sent to the work units to which the villagers belong, and the leaders of the work units will give a score to each of their employees. The forms will then be collected and reviewed by each Party branch, and the Party will also send the head of each villager's team to randomly inspect the families. The final results will be submitted to the Labor Resource Office, which will distribute welfare benefits to each person

[37] The Chinese Central Government allows, and sometimes even encourages, villages to have their own codes of conduct as a more effective way of grassroots management, as long as the regulations are not contradictory to the state laws.

[38] They cannot get back the exact lot of land they had when the household responsibility system was enacted in the village, because the village's layout has been redesigned according to the collective needs. The lot of land they get will be decided by the village administration, usually at the outskirts of the village.

[39] The star of new culture (*xinfeng xing*) requires villagers to quit any superstitious activities, lavish rituals, funerals, weddings, and cults and sexist practices, which are traditionally common in rural China, and to respect others' religious beliefs, while not participating in any illegal religious practices.

[40] Nanjie Archives keeps a copy of the "Detailed Regulations on the Criteria for the Ten-Star Model Family Contest in Nanjie Village."

accordingly. In addition to monetary sanction, in a closely knit community like Nanjie, people being punished also "lose face" in public. Therefore, although it may not cost the villagers much economically to have a star deducted, it hurts emotionally and morally.

Although Nanjie is good at mitigating rural inequality and the peasants' burden prevalent in other villages, some problems remain unresolved. Clearly, democracy is not strongly emphasized in Nanjie Village, although villagers and Party members do vote for their committee members. The core of the leadership has been pretty consistent over the years. Even though villagers enjoy a high degree of economic privilege, they are, in turn, deprived of much political power. Especially in such a collective, different voices may be suppressed because of the redistribution mechanism. As shown by the Code of Conduct and the association between the ten-star model family contest and welfare benefits, nonconformists are punished. Even if some people want to disengage from the collective, the village will not be able to give back their own land, for the land is collectively owned and operated now and the whole village layout cannot be changed. Therefore, there is the constant struggle between personal interests and collective interests. Even the smallest dissatisfaction with the system may lead people to doubt the benefits of collective ownership. It is said that some villagers have pressured Wang Hongbin to give back their share of land, citing the CCP Central Committee's policy of the household responsibility system (He 2006).

However, the regulations, as we learn from Erwei's case, are not as strictly enforced as they were in the 1990s when class struggle meetings were held frequently. His father still works in the village, and he himself also lives in the apartment distributed by the village. The village will also assign a piece of land to those disengaged from the collective. As I walked around the village with Lü Xiaohu on my third visit to Nanjie, I saw a small plot of land farmed by villagers individually, and there were also traditional rural brick houses built by villagers themselves on the outskirts of the village close to the Chaoyang Gate, which were not as modern as the apartment buildings built by the village. Apparently, they belong to people who no longer believe in the communal lifestyle. Villagers and migrant workers alike tell me that there are fewer meetings than before. For villagers, the well-known "struggle meetings" (*douzheng hui*), or "criticism and self-criticism meetings," are no longer held that frequently. For migrant workers, moral education is not as heavily emphasized as the acquisition of skill training. Except for the occasional recitals of Mao's works, and singing revolutionary songs before and after work, there are hardly any meetings or learning sessions on Mao Zedong Thought as indicated in the previous literature on Nanjie. Is the relaxation of political and ideological control a compromise with reality, as ideological consensus becomes second to economic competition?

Another real threat to the square Nanjie adheres to is corruption. The success of a community lies in its social integration. However, Nanjie, after all, is not isolated from the larger society, especially considering that its high level of industrialization requires full contact with, and active participation in, the outside world. As Nanjie's equality is mainly defined in economic terms, people with more power may seek to convert political means into economic gains, and thus economic equality can no longer be maintained as before. Erwei told me that, although before the year 2000, the village had been great in all respects, corruption was becoming rampant. Pointing to the popcorn maker in front of him, he said that Nanjie is exactly like it – looks clean from the outside but is dark inside. However, even a dissident like him agrees that Wang Hongbin is very devoted to the village and is not corrupt, but things can get out of his control. Mr. Zhao, a Beijie villager who sells popcorn outside the Chaoyang Gate, also agreed that Wang is good, but "one person," he said, "can't save the collective." No matter how exaggerated their accounts might be, several scandals are widely known among villagers and even non-villagers.

Corruption in Nanjie is twofold. First, some villagers who have access to power or collective resources sacrifice collective interests for personal gain. For example, originally all the gifts villagers received with regard to businesses were supposed to be handed over to the village, but now some people just keep them as personal belongings. A village accountant even embezzled collective money into a personal account to seek the higher interest on the black market (*chi gaoxi*). The cashier of the Agriculture Bank, who offered the high interest, later took the money and disappeared. The biggest scandal is probably that of the number 3 figure in the village, Wang Hongbin's right-hand man, Wang Jinzhong. Before his sudden death of excessive drinking in 2003, Wang Jinzhong, a major contributor to Nanjie's development, was head of the Villagers' Committee, vice president and vice managing director of the Nanjie Corporate Group. He went to Beijing with Wang Hongbin to sign the contract with the Jingsong Pastry Factory in 1984. Many officials from Linying county and Luohe city attended his funeral to pay him their respects. According to Lü Xiaohu, because of Nanjie's close relations with the military, several generals also attended the funeral, and the funeral procession included more than 200 cars.

However, a woman with a child appeared shortly after the funeral and claimed that they should inherit Wang's belongings and enjoy Nanjie residency. It was not until then that people discovered that this highly respected man actually had a mistress (*bao ernai*). Rumor also has it that, when packing up the belongings of the deceased, Wang Hongbin was so shocked to see a safe with 20 million yuan and a house ownership certificate that he almost fainted. Although Wang Hongbin denied that Wang Jinzhong had personal deposits, he admitted that he had a mistress and bought a house for her. Soon afterward, Wang Hongbin initiated a three-session campaign (*sanhui huodong*) – that is, the learning session (*xuexi hui*), the small-group session (*shenghuo hui*), and the evaluation session (*pingyi hui*) – the theme of which was to say no to mistresses, excessive drinking,[41] bribery, and the abuse of power and to have a village-wide discussion of money, power, and status. The village also takes stricter measures to audit the balance sheets of each enterprise, and every quarter, accountants are rotated among enterprises to reduce their power and prevent corruption.

Not only villagers but also employees from outside the village can erode the collective economy. Some senior managers, who were hired at very high salaries, left Nanjie once they had profiteered in the village. Some were outright cheaters that conned the village out of millions of dollars. After all, whether Nanjie is a success or a failure has nothing to do with their lives as in the infamous story of the perpetual motion machine project that caused Nanjie a loss of 16 million yuan.[42] Such incidents are especially harmful because they are a damaging blow not only to Nanjie's economy, but also to the villagers' trust in outsiders. Nanjie's development needs talent from

---

[41] Drinking liquor is part of Henan's culture. Many people drink liquor with every meal. They have also invented various ways of toasting. For example, the host or the inferior should pour wine into the cups and hand them to the guest or the superior to show his/her respect, and the guest should bottom up three times. Also when a fish dish is on the table, the person whose seat faces the fish head should drink three cups of liquor and facing the fish tail means four cups.

[42] The perpetual motion machine project was introduced to Nanjie by people who claimed to be scientists, one of whom was said to be an American PhD. They brought newspaper stories and other video clips to prove that other places were also experimenting on the machine. Wang Hongbin, a junior high school graduate, obviously had no idea of the laws of thermodynamics and believed that a machine could actually be produced that could bring Nanjie millions in profits. He sent people to Shenzhen to see the scientist's product, a perpetual motion automobile, and was thus convinced of its viability. Despite that all the other twenty members of the leadership disagreed with the project, Wang decided to invest in the research and development. Of course, later the project proved to be a failure, and Wang criticized himself in the village meeting (Liu 2004: 158–161, 182). Wang learned his lesson and stated that in the future he would hear more from the masses to make correct decisions. He admitted that this was the biggest mistake he had ever made during his terms in office. Since this incident, all the new projects have to be fully discussed among Party Committee members and assessed by experts. Some argue that this incident indicates that Wang's personal power is too high (Lu 2004).

other places, but if outsiders are deemed untrustworthy, they will not be given equal opportunities and benefits, and it will then be less likely that they would want to contribute to Nanjie's growth and prosperity. In this way, a vicious cycle can be set in motion. On the other hand, it also shows the weaknesses in Nanjie's recruiting and decision-making procedures.

Circle on the outside also means competition in the marketplace. The village enterprises are not as profitable as in their golden days. A direct indicator is the decrease in the number of migrant workers in recent years, which is partly a result of a higher level of mechanization, but more importantly, a result of the declining profits. According to Mr. Zhang, director of the Corporate Management Office (*qiguan ban*), the number of migrant workers in Nanjie reached some 12,000 people in 1997 but has subsequently dropped to about 7,000 each year; the total industrial output dropped from 1.6 billion yuan in 1997 – the highest in its history – to 1.2 billion yuan in 2002, not adjusting for inflation, and after the structural reform in 2004[43] it picked up again to 1.5 billion yuan in 2008. Profits of the star enterprises such as instant noodles and the beer factories have all shrunk and so have the villagers' welfare benefits, although only to a very small extent. In restructuring the economy from traditional food-processing industries to more technical and capital-intensive industries such as electrical appliances, thermo-power, pharmaceuticals, real estates, and more recently, green products such as degradable plastic bags, Nanjie is at a turning point, and Wang Hongbin calls it "starting a new undertaking" (*erci chuangye*). Mr. Zhang told me that the pharmaceutical plant Nanjie acquired in Luohe city was doing fine, but the other pharmaceutical company, Quanwei Pharmaceutical, was stagnant because of a lack of capital. As a result of the state's macroeconomic control, it is now harder to get bank loans. Gu Yi also commented that given its location, Nanjie still had a problem marketing its high-end products and sales of such products remained mediocre.

Apparently the circle on the outside provides the square inside the village with economic resources that can maintain the high level of social welfare and the equality of distribution. However, it also confronts the square with ethical challenges and economic competition. As villagers are exposed to global consumerism, it can be difficult to keep the boundary between the

---

[43] Before the structural reform, the general manager of the corporate group, party secretary Wang Hongbin, was in charge of all the major decisions, but after the reform, all the village enterprises were grouped into six sectors, with six deputy general managers, each in charge of one sector. This marked the partial separation of village and corporate management in Nanjie.

circle and the square, as the economic sphere cannot be separated from ideological, social, and political forces. Therefore, the future of the village lies in the interactive dynamics between the circle and the square. The square will lose its ground to the circle unless it can prove to be an integrative force, a more effective way to organize both the economy and the society.

Despite the economic recession and the many problems facing Nanjie, it seems that Wang Hongbin wants to reassure the villagers, and the rest of the nation, that Nanjie is still striving to develop into a communist community. In a middle and upper management meeting I observed in August 2006, Wang Hongbin claimed that a one-year training program for communist theories would be held from early September 2006. Party and village cadres and the managers of the corporations should all attend the program. Another fifty people would be selected from each corporation, and twenty people would be admitted to the program from outside of Nanjie. Except for the cadres and managers, all other people should attend the program on a full-time basis. It remains to be seen whether such programs can reinforce Nanjie's current institutions and social cohesion.

### A Political Conspiracy?

As I talked to a retired senior official and scholar, who provided me with access to Huaxi Village in Jiangsu province in 2006, I asked, out of curiosity, what he thought of Nanjie Village. He answered without a second thought that Nanjie was not on the right track and Nanjie would fail. However, to my surprise, he had not even been to Nanjie. Why was he so sure of something that he had not seen for himself, while I still did not know if I could give a fair evaluation of Nanjie after my three visits? Thinking that probably he was not alone in negating Nanjie without actually seeing how it works, I started to wonder if Nanjie, as a so-called leftist model, is more than a rural community. My concern was reinforced by several officers from Xuchang People's Armed Forces Department (*Renwu Bu*).[44] They thought that Nanjie has not abided by the laws of development. When I asked if by the laws of development they meant market laws, they answered they were referring to every law. They said that Nanjie was mainly supported by the Henan Armed Police Force Detachment and some leftist leaders, such as Zhang Aiping, a general and senior Chinese leader who died in 2003. According to them,

[44] Xuchang is a city in Henan province that borders Luohe. Linying county used to be under Xuchang's jurisdiction and was not assigned to Luohe until very recently. Therefore, many people in Nanjie, or Linying, have more affinity with Xuchang than to Luohe, and it is actually easier for Nanjie villagers to go to downtown Xuchang than to downtown Luohe.

there will not be a second Nanjie in China, overlooking the fact that there are other villages on a similar path both in Henan and in other provinces, although they may not use Maoism as their founding ideology.

Politically speaking, Nanjie satisfies two functions. First, its role as a star village can be seen as one of the achievements of local officials at the county, municipal, and provincial levels. Therefore, whether it can succeed and maintain its record is not just the concern of the village, but also that of the upper-level administrations, and they will all help to keep its momentum and provide it with preferential policies and economic resources such as loans and reduced taxes, unless some new stars occur and become more resplendent than Nanjie. Second, it serves as a stronghold for the leftists, who still believe in Marxism, Maoism, and the advantages of communism over capitalism, but at the same time it also becomes the target for the rightists' criticism and skepticism. That is perhaps why the central government neither promotes the Nanjie model nor suppresses it, although Nanjie seems to be extremely anachronistic in transitional China.

However, for the villagers and several villages that are imitating Nanjie's path such as the neighboring Beixu and Longtang Villages, proving political points is probably not their primary goal, except when it can be converted into substantial political and economic capital. Besides, when Nanjie first embarked on the path to industrialization through collective ownership and equal distribution, it was mostly guided by its own judgment of the economic and political circumstances. Its unprecedented economic progress drew attention from the upper-level administrations, and this enhanced its political networks and external economic support including access to bank loans for its various projects and collective enterprises and opportunities for setting up joint ventures.

## Some Final Comments

At the end of this chapter, I would like to make some final comments on the validity and problems with the Nanjie model and its implications. These discussions are also relevant to the next chapter, the case of Huaxi Village, as both villages share some similar social structures.

### On Mao Zedong Thought and Nanjie

Many newspaper reports and articles on Nanjie emphasize its distinct communist ideology. Some argue that this is the glue that holds Nanjiers together, while others think it is simply a show put on for those who want to see. I think it can be both and neither. It is a way of mobilizing social, economic, and political capital that the local community needs.

First of all, it provides ideological support and cohesion to a collective economy. Nanjie was once privatized, and the land was not fully re-collectivized until 1990, and the economy was not collectivized until 1994. Besides, Nanjie villagers had a tradition of being involved in small businesses. How then to legitimize collectivism when the market has brought about new opportunities and the state supports deeper reform in the rural area? Mao Zedong Thought provides theories to justify Nanjie's practices. According to the person who is in charge of compiling Nanjie's village history, when Nanjie implemented Mao Zedong Thought as its guiding ideology, the three volumes of *Deng Xiaoping Theory* had not been published yet, and the only complete theory was Mao's. For people growing up in the commune era, no matter whether they are literate, Mao's works are probably the most familiar, as they used to recite them everyday. It was actually in Xinxiang, Henan, about 200 kilometers north of Nanjie, where Mao spoke highly of the People's Commune in 1958.

In addition, Nanjie Village is not a natural village (*zirancun*). According to a survey in 2005, there were 84 surnames in Nanjie, although Wang (18.58 percent), Zhang (11.61 percent), Li (10.57 percent), and Zhao (5.8 percent) were among the major surnames.[45] Villagers also have different religious beliefs. There is a mosque and a temple in the village, which have become scenic spots in the village park, and a church further north of the main settlements. As a result, Mao Zedong Thought has become the substitute for family and kinship ties and an overarching value, a religion in the Durkheimian sense, because "Essentially, it is nothing other than a body of collective beliefs and practices endowed with a certain authority" (Durkheim 1973: 51). That collective interests should have priority over personal interests or family interests is the most dominant value. It is constantly reinforced by artifacts with symbolic meanings like the slogans and various propaganda media and through activities or "rituals" such as singing revolutionary songs, reciting Mao's works, and attending group meetings.

Second, it creates a unique community identity for the village and the villagers. When many other villages have moved on to adopt new state policies and ideas, Nanjie chose to stick to Mao Zedong Thought, which is still officially recognized by the CCP as the root for Deng Xiaoping Theory and

---

[45] The manuscript of the village history, copied in 2006.

Jiang Zemin's Three Represents (*sange daibiao*)[46] theory, although in many senses, it has become increasingly nominal. It tells the villagers and outsiders alike that Nanjie is different, thus creating a boundary. Community members have more reason and responsibilities to protect their collective identity and reputation; on the other hand, a past ideology can also serve as an effective way of mobilizing resources, as all people who have sympathy toward the ideology are welcomed to join – a way of expanding networks. That is why Nanjie has received support from leftists in the CCP and attracted those who are nostalgic for the past or idealistic about the future.

Third, as a collective economy develops and prospers, Mao Zedong Thought or the goal of building a communist community can draw economic resources as well. It can, first, grant Nanjie a label of being trustworthy, as the village enterprises are collectively owned and the villagers aim to build a communist heaven. The reputation of being honest and idealistic can offset Nanjie's weakness as a rural corporation when doing business with urban enterprises. Because the distinctive feature has drawn attention from upper-level governments and reporters worldwide, it can also bring about favorable policies, priority in low-interest bank loans as well as business opportunities. A direct conversion of cultural capital into economic capital is through red tourism, which brings in a steady cash flow to the village and further promotes Nanjie's distinctiveness. As a result, the cultural capital, social capital, and economic capital interact to reinforce one another.

### On Collectivism and Nanjie

Scholars have long questioned the incentives for the efficient use of communal assets under a common property resource (CPR) regime. Hardin (1968), about four decades ago, proposed the "tragedy of the commons," saying that an asset held under a CPR regime is inherently inefficient, because individuals do not get proper incentives to act in a socially efficient and responsible way. The result is free riding and over-exploitation. Gordon (1954) also has a scathing comment on common property; in his words, "Everybody's property is nobody's property. Wealth that is free for all is valued by none …" This has become a classical critique of communalism and socialism. For those scholars, the solution to the problems or tragedies of common property is to either privatize the property or establish state control and management through what Hardin calls "mutual coercion."

---

[46] The three represents are represent advanced social productive forces, represent the progressive development of China's advanced culture, and represent the fundamental interests of the majority.

An increasing number of scholars, however, argue that through decentralized collective management of CPRs by their users, like the cooperatives, the "tragedy of the commons" can be overcome (Wade 1988; Berkes 1989). Some specialists, by analyzing developing countries, posit that local institutional arrangements such as customs and social conventions can induce cooperative actions and that common property regimes can be more effective than state and private property arrangements (Gibbs and Bromley 1989; Ostrom 1990). Critics also argue that Hardin confuses common property with no property or open access. The tragedy of the commons results not from the inherent defects of the collective property system, but from institutional failure to control access or enforce internal decisions for collective use. The institutional failure can be a result of either internal reasons, such as members neglecting to manage themselves, or external reasons, such as state intervention, market penetration, and other intrusions of outsiders (Berkes and Folke 1998).

Collectivism in Nanjie is expressed in its communal use of land and collective operation of enterprises. To institutionalize collectivism, the village has created its own mechanisms including moral education based on communist ideologies and traditional norms, a multiple incentive system that integrates economic incentive and sociopolitical pressure, and a patriarchal governance structure.

I have discussed the ideological aspect in the previous section. Profit making and industrialization are justified by seeking public good and equality among villagers. For the incentive structure, economic rewards are minimal in Nanjie, as differentiation in income is very little and salaries are almost fixed. However, since the development of the collective economy is correlated with the social welfare benefits that villagers can enjoy, there is still some economic incentive, as the bigger the cake, the larger the slice one can receive. The free-riding problem may still exist, but it is mitigated by a combination of peer pressure and the boundary set between villagers and non-villagers. Therefore, collective interests are not empty words but indeed involve various stakes and commitments that the villagers have put in. Both profits and risks are shared among members. Moreover, in a collective environment, there is also the incentive of gaining respect and acknowledgment from other members, similar to what Offer (1997) calls an "economy of regard."

The patriarchal system routinizes charismatic authority and stabilizes the collective model. Wang Hongbin, as the political and spiritual leader of the village, controls who will be selected into the leadership. Although village and Party Committee members are elected, important positions in the village enterprises and administration are appointed by the Party, and mostly by Wang. This screening process ensures that administrators in Nanjie's corporations agree with the collectivist norms, and the collective economy is under the Party guidance and community members' supervision. Therefore, no matter which village enterprise one is in charge of, he or she has to integrate market mechanisms with the collectivist culture of the village. This adds the political incentive for villagers who want to be promoted to positions with more challenges, responsibilities, and power, as human capital alone cannot grant the elite position.

The validity of Nanjie's collective model lies in its protection of the underprivileged peasants and its ability to pool economic, social, and political resources. As the state's reform and opening-up policy brings in market mechanisms, many peasants are not prepared for market competition. In the meantime, agriculture alone cannot provide peasants with subsistence in many areas. Instead of counting on individual abilities, the collective model offers a safety net. It accelerates rural urbanization and industrialization, as the collective economy is based on redistribution, and the development of the infrastructure, health care, education, and other public goods are given priority.

There are several cases where villagers, who left the collective and worked on their own, eventually came back. For example, Geng Fujie, who used to be the managing director of the Nanjie Corporate Group, resigned and left Nanjie in 2002, as his suggestion of changing the Corporate Group's ownership form from collective to a shareholding system was refused by Wang Hongbin. The same year, Chen Shuxin, director of the spices factory, a very competent entrepreneur, left the village without a word, because he was outraged by the village's punishment for his "unnecessary" dining. He opened his own spices company. However, they both failed at running their own businesses and rejoined Nanjie's collective economy. Geng is now the vice managing director of the village's Dili Electric Appliances Corporation. Those individuals were regarded by the villagers as "capable" people, but they failed in open market competition.[47] These cases have become a warning to those who are thinking of leaving and a reassurance to those who have stayed.

On the other hand, collective networks can make the enterprises more competitive. The initial funding of the first two enterprises in Nanjie, about

---

[47]  Based on my interview with Qu Yuhong and Nanjie's archived documents.

180,000 yuan, came from the personal savings of cadres and Party members combined with the support from their friends and relatives (Liu 2004). Later on, as collective enterprises, it was easier to get bank loans. The emphasis on collective interests also leaves the village enterprises with more capital to reinvest and the village more funds to build its infrastructure, as labor costs are low and fixed. The various business opportunities are the result of mobilizing the networks with Nanjiers who work in other regions and their personal contacts. Moreover, as a collective, the village enterprise is at a better position bargaining with the state and upper-level governments for preferential policies.

Unlike what many people assume, Nanjie is not a black box where nobody knows what is going on; nor is it a utopia where nothing could go wrong. In fact, it is quite accessible to visitors, and it has full contact with the outside world as a result of modern technologies such as the Internet and TV. One does not need a special permit to get into the village, which is different from Huaxi Village that I will discuss in the next chapter, and most of the villagers are very willing to talk. As a slogan in Nanjie indicates, "Nanjie's friends are all over the world," suggesting that it fully understands the importance of social capital in the marketplace. No matter whether one agrees or disagrees with the model, it welcomes people to come and take a look at it themselves. In this sense, the kind of collectivism in Nanjie is different from the collectivism in the Maoist era. Nanjie has become increasingly open and tolerant to various values over the years, and villagers can choose to leave and return to the community. Small changes such as from the distribution of food and other products each month to the allocation of "welfare coupons (*fuli quan*) with which villagers can choose things they like at the village supermarkets also indicates the penetration of the market and the transformation of the village's own institutions. However, Mao Zedong Thought, with its emphasis on collective interests over private interests, has not changed.

How well it can adapt to a more competitive market, as the fiscal reform in the state leaves Nanjie with no special privileges in getting loans; how long the leadership can sustain villagers' trust and respect; and how much the collective's ability to innovate – not just the wisdom of a few cadres – can be utilized will determine the future of the village. Wang Hongbin himself is also aware of the structural holes in Nanjie's system, and Nanjie is only a village searching for its path of development, not a myth or a legend. For the time being, the villagers are used to the social welfare benefits and are dependent on the collective system. Despite all the doubts, disbeliefs, criticism as well as new challenges including the fiscal crisis, industrial upgrading, and the media coverage in 2008 saying that Nanjie had de facto become privatized,[48] the village is moving ahead, continuing its search.

[48] In 2008 several newspapers in China including *Southern Metropolis Daily* (*Nanfang Dushi Bao*) reported that as early as 2004 Nanjie Corporate Group was no longer collectively owned, as several cadres headed by Wang Hongbin became the shareholders of the collective property; therefore, Nanjie had actually been privatized. See, for example, Shangguan Jiaoming, "The Truth of the Development of the 'Red Hundred Million Yuan Village' Nanjie" ('Hongse Yiyuancun' Henan Nanjiecun de Fazhan Zhenxiang) (*Southern Metropolis Daily*, Feb. 26, 2008). However, based on my interviews in 2010 and several other reports including Wang Shouguo, Li Weihua, Wang Lufeng, and Liu Guangchao, "Investigating Nanjie's Change of Ownership: 'The Economy is Slowly Reviving' after a Difficult Self-Rescue" (Nanjie zhi Bian Diaocha: Jiannan Zijiu hou 'Jingji zheng Fusu') (*Dahe Daily*, March 17, 2008), nothing has changed in terms of ownership. The villagers and administrators also claimed that the reporter from *Southern Metropolis* had never been to Nanjie to investigate and that they have already protested to the Henan provincial government. As the village hit an economic bottom in 2004, a brokerage firm in Shenzhen, Guangdong province, suggested that Nanjie could raise funds in the capital market, but to go public, they had to put collective property under private names, so Wang Hongbin and five other cadres became the nominal sharcholders out of strategic concerns. I was told that they signed at the same time another agreement that all the property was still collectively owned and they could not take it as their private property. Of course, Nanjie ended up not going public, so transformation to a shareholding system never occurred.

THREE

# Socialism with Huaxi Characteristics

The sky of Huaxi is the sky of the Communist Party,
The land of Huaxi is the land of socialism,
...
Socialism can definitely defeat capitalism.
                    Lyrics from the *Huaxi Village Song*

The Chinese state labels its development strategy "socialism with Chinese characteristics." To many, it is indeed capitalism in disguise. Anything with Chinese characteristics has almost become a euphemistic way of confirming exceptionalism or justifying paradoxes. Nonetheless, such a label can be readily understood by sociologists, as each society is unique in its own sense, and boundaries between different social systems are often fluid, hence the discussion over varieties of capitalism and socialism. Huaxi Village, also known as the "No. 1 Village under the Heaven" (*tianxia diyi cun*), is located in Jiangsu province fifty miles away from Shanghai, one of the most developed regions in China (Map 3.1). As the wealthiest village in China, it has been honored by the central government as a model to be emulated in the construction of China's "new socialist countryside" (*shehuizhuyi xin nongcun*),[1] the latest campaign by the Hu regime to reinvigorate China's deprived rural areas and mitigate the rural-urban divide. Every day hundreds of visitors gather in Huaxi to witness its development and learn from its experience.

---

[1] The new socialist countryside is, according to the Central Government, characterized by enhanced production (*shengchan fazhan*), high living standards (*shenghuo fuyu*), a healthy rural culture (*xiangfeng wenming*), a neat and clean village layout (*cunrong zhengjie*), and democratic management (*guanli minzhu*).

Map 3.1. Location of Huaxi Village.

## A Brief Village History

Although located in southern Jiangsu province, a region known as a land of fish and rice (*yumi zhixiang*), similar to Nanjie, Huaxi used to be a poor village with rugged, muddy roads and barren soil. There was a local folksong that captures some of its earlier character: "The highland looks like a bamboo hat (*douli*), and the lowland resembles a wok floating in a pool (*yuguotang*)." The highest farmland was about 13 feet above the lowest, making it extremely difficult to plan and farm. That was how Huaxi appeared more than 40 years ago.

Huaxi Village was called the "Leap Forward Brigade" during the late 1950s and early 1960s[2] and was in charge of ten production teams (Wan 2001). The present village was officially created in 1961 when the 17th Brigade of the Huashu People's Commune was divided into four parts, merging twelve natural villages (*zirancun*). It was named Huaxi because it is located in the western part of the Huashu People's Commune ("*xi*" means west in Chinese). At that time, the village was rather small with a fairly low output and income. Four decades later, however, it has grown into an area with more than 30,000 people and an annual per capita income of US$8,000, 19 times higher than the national average for peasants.[3] Visitors at home and abroad were impressed by its rows of European-style houses with their state-of-the-art equipment and decorations, parks with famous scenes from all over the world, pagoda-style hotels, and bustling factories. In a word, it looks more like American suburbia or a Disney theme park than a traditional Chinese village (Figure 3.1).

Similar to Nanjie, Huaxi also has a story of development full of sweat, tears, and even some blood. When Huaxi was first formed in 1961, it was during the Three Years of Natural Disaster, one of the hardest times in Communist China when a large number of people died from hunger and malnutrition. Wu Renbao, the party secretary of the 17th Brigade, became the party secretary of Huaxi Village (Brigade). He has been in that position for 43 years and did not retire until 2003 when he decided to step down, and his youngest son was elected as the new party secretary. However, he remains active in the village's economic and social affairs. His new position is director of the village's General Office (*zongban*),[4] and he remains to be a member of the Standing Committee of the Village Party Committee. I will return to this later. The point is that the village's history is inseparable from Wu's personal biography.

---

[2]  The Great Leap Forward was an economic and social plan initiated by Mao to use China's vast population to rapidly transform mainland China from a primarily agrarian economy into a modern, industrialized communist society from 1958 to 1962.

[3]  When Huaxi was first formed, it only had an area of 845 mu (139 acres) and a population of 667. With an annual grain output of merely 681 jin (750 pounds) per mu, the village had an accumulated collective fund of 1,764 yuan and a debt of 15,000 yuan. Every villager received 53 yuan per year (Feng 1995). In 2005, however, Huaxi grew into a village of 30 square kilometers (7,413 acres) and more than 30,000 villagers, with an annual sales revenue of 30 billion yuan (US$3.7 billion), and fixed assets worth of over 4 billion yuan (US$500 million).

[4]  The General Office is a new administrative entity established by Wu to supervise the Village Party Committee.

Figure 3.1. Residential houses in Huaxi from the top of the Golden Pagoda Hotel. Photo by the author.
*Note*: There are at least five generations of houses in Huaxi built in different years with different square footages and designs that reflect the time of their construction. When I revisited Huaxi in 2010, the exterior of the older houses (the ones that occupy most of the picture) had been repainted.

When Wu became the party secretary of Huaxi, the initial task facing him was to feed the weak and hungry villagers. Wu realized that to raise the grain output, they first needed to develop industries to acquire money for agricultural investment. At that time Xiangyang Village, to the north of Huaxi, was selling a big millstone to survive the famine. Wu decided to buy it, for it could on the one hand, save labor when everybody hardly had any extra energy for milling their own flour, and on the other hand, bring extra revenue to the village by processing flour and fodder. Therefore, he borrowed money to buy the millstone and carried the more-than-1,400-pound grinder back to the village with the help of seven other villagers.

The next challenge was to build a mill for the millstone – but where to find the bricks? Villagers started to see Wu carrying a bamboo basket on his back to collect stones and bricks on the road and near the river. Soon the villagers followed suit. However, there was still a big deficit. After tearing down a deserted village temple dedicated to the God of Earth (*tudi miao*), they were still short of bricks. Then Wu heard that a neighboring village, Zhouzhuang Village,[5] was selling three old houses. Borrowing money wherever he could, he was finally able to pay for the houses and get enough bricks for the mill. An old water buffalo driving the millstone in a shabby mill marks the start of Huaxi's industrialization.

When the 17th Brigade was broken down to four brigades, Huaxi acquired a thirty-horsepower diesel engine. However, it was not until 1963, when Huaxi's economic conditions were improving, that the engine began to play its role in production. That year Wu hired Huaxi's first talented technician, Zha Abing, to operate the machine, and Zha helped train two Huaxi villagers as apprentices. In this way, the water buffalo was replaced by the diesel engine. To make full use of the engine, Wu and the technicians bought another millstone and attached it to the machine. At that time the daily output was only 600 jin (approximately 660 pounds) of flour. Wu then purchased a small power generator, and thanks to the diesel engine, the mill and brigade office building had electricity – a great achievement for an agrarian community.

Of course, then the story goes on: stone mills were replaced by steel mills, and the output of flour was quadrupled in 1965, reaching 2500 jin, the mill turned into the Huaxi Grain and Fodder Processing Factory with a net profit of more than 5,000 yuan (US$710) a year. Since then, a series of factories have opened in Huaxi.

In conformity with the ideology of the CCP, Huaxi's leadership also believed in man's power to transform and remake nature through hard work and the formulation of meticulous yet bold plans. On February 10, 1964, the *People's Daily* published an article, "The Path of Dazhai Village" (*Dazhai Zhilu*) (Song and Fan), promoting Dazhai as a model for converting the barren mountainous area into productive farmland. Since then, a campaign was started nationwide to learn from Dazhai's experience. Wu was also inspired and encouraged by the news story. He and the other cadres and village representatives paid site visits to the twelve natural villages in the village, measuring farmland and investigating rivers. There were more than 1,300 plots of separated farmland, and more than 40 water streams and pools, which were detrimental to Huaxi's agricultural development. Soon after this, Wu Renbao came up with The Fifteen-Year Prospective Plan on How the Huaxi

---

[5]   Not the Zhouzhuang Town, which has become a well-known tourist attraction with waters and bridges.

Brigade Should Learn from Dazhai (*Huaxi Dadui Xue Dazhai Shiwu Nian Fazhan Yuanjing Guihua*), a blueprint to transform Huaxi's landscape by 1979 in three five-year stages.

The plan was summarized into Five Goals (*Wuge Yi*) for the convenience of promoting it to the villagers: (1) adopt a socialist perspective that loves the country and the collective; (2) excavate a Huaxi River for both irrigation and drainage; (3) build an area of farmland with a high and stable output through water and land management; (4) create an annual grain output of one ton per mu; (5) build a new socialist village.[6] In the end, Huaxi reached the objectives of the plan 7 years earlier than the designated date, despite the adverse political environment during the Cultural Revolution.

There are two unusual things about Huaxi's history. First, Huaxi has always been a model, no matter whether in Maoist China as a more agrarian community, or in the present day as a fully industrialized village. Huaxi is probably the most enduring model village in China. Second, unlike Nanjie, Huaxi has never divided its land, nor have the village enterprises ever been privatized, not even when the household responsibility system was supposed to be the prescription for rural development and when the once popular TVEs in southern Jiangsu faded into obscurity. A critical question concerns the amount of pressure from the upper-level administrations to conform and how the village leadership dealt with it. Mr. Qü, one of the twenty-three deputy party secretaries in Huaxi, told me that there was definitely pressure from above, but the village leaders were able to endure it (*dingzhe*), and the higher government officials had no alternative but to accept what Huaxi was doing, because "we did better than those who divided their land. In addition, we already had village enterprises, and peasants only did their farming after they finished their jobs in the factories. They [meaning the higher level officials] couldn't complain about anything."

Since the founding of the People's Republic of China (PRC), there have always been models set by the central government and different levels of the administration for others to emulate. Partly because China is such a large country, it is unwise to implement policies without first testing them in a few areas. It is also because a successful case can be useful for political bargaining. Local governments can be at a more advantageous position to compete for the scarce economic, political, and social resources needed for local development. The upper-level administrations, on the other hand, will

---

[6] Notice that Wu included "building a new socialist village" into his plan as early as 1964, while the central government proposed to build a new socialist countryside in 2005 and set it up as one of the primary objectives for China's 11th Five Year Plan in 2006.

allocate resources to the lower levels according to their political priorities, and creating examples of good practice can thus justify their policies.

Dealing with pressure from the upper levels of the political structure is easier said than done. When Huaxi's grain output per mu reached 1200 jin in 1966, it became one of the five model brigades in Jiangyin county. However, being a model did not just mean honor, it also brought about more inspections from senior authorities. On the one hand, Huaxi received greater attention; on the other hand, it became a place for the upper-level administrators to promote and spread their policies and plans, some of which might not be practical for Huaxi. Once a group of officials came to Huaxi to check its manure collection and asked Wu Renbao to take the lead in applying 400 *dan* (about 44,000 pounds) of basal manure to each mu of land. However, Wu refused. He thought that was ineffective and inefficient and a waste of time and energy, and he said he could not let other brigades follow this stupid measure. After several other similar incidents, Wu irritated those officials, and they accused him of arrogance and complacency. They also criticized him for giving priority to Huaxi's own Fifteen Year Plan rather than the county's big plan. Soon Huaxi was no longer the model for the county. However, 6 months later, those officials went back to Huaxi, because although other brigades were more obedient, Huaxi could claim much greater achievements. Wu Renbao also learned not to directly confront the officials' orders but to accept what the officials said to their faces, yet not to carry them out, if they were unsuitable for Huaxi (Feng 1995; Wu 2004).

When most of the rural areas had adopted the household responsibility system promoted in China by 1982, Huaxi maintained its collective ownership. At that time, Huaxi had already transformed itself from a purely agrarian production system to a mixed economy, and industrial revenue accounted for 80 percent of its total income. By 1981, Huaxi's collective assets had reached 700,000 yuan (roughly US$100,000), and its per capita annual income was about 1500 yuan (more than $200) (Pang 2006).

In 1985 a conference was held in Shunwai Village in Nanchang City, about 480 miles southwest of Shanghai, and the participants comprised the six most well-known model villages at the time, including Liuzhuang in Henan, Daqiuzhuang in Tianjin, and Huaxi. Huaxi representatives were shocked by the achievements of Daqiuzhuang. Although Huaxi had a higher per capita income, the total economic output was far less than that produced at Daqiuzhuang.[7] In August that year, Wu Renbao led eighty cadres and party

---

[7] Daqiuzhuang had a total output of more than 30 million yuan (more than US$4 million) in 1983.

members to make a pledge in front of the Martyrs' Memorial Monument in Nanjing to build Huaxi into a 100-million-yuan village within 3 years. If the goal was not reached by 1988, all their personal assets would be given to the village. Each of the eighty people signed the agreement.

During the next 3 years, taking advantage of its geographical location, Huaxi established several joint ownership enterprises with large state-owned businesses in Shanghai. In 1985, the Huaxi Copper and Aluminum Material Factory was established, in partnership with the Shanghai Copper Factory. Three years later, the factory received a production permit from the China Nonferrous Metal General Company. Meanwhile, the Huaxi Forging Factory was put into production in 1986, producing flange plates, and its products were exported through the Shanghai Hardware and Machinery General Company. In the same year, the Huaxi Aluminum Products Factory was built using 600,000 yuan raised from villager stock ownership. By 1988, the Huaxi Agro-Industrial-Commercial Combines oversaw twenty-three factories, three companies, two hotels, a shop, a construction team, a transportation team, and four poultry and fish raising farms, and its combined output passed 100 million yuan.

The Huaxi Group Corporation was officially launched in 1994, replacing the Huaxi Agro-Industrial-Commercial Combines. It consisted of eight companies manufacturing steel and building materials, chemical fibers, nonferrous metals, woolen products, garments, and providing real estate and travel services. In 1999, Huaxi Village A-stock was listed on the Shenzhen Stock Exchange, raising 290 million yuan (more than US$35 million using the 1999 exchange rate) in its initial public offering (IPO). That was the first time a village enterprise ever went public. To meet the growing demand for land stimulated by industrial development and also as a way to boost the economy of the neighboring villages, Huaxi merged sixteen villages between 2001 and 2004, to become Huaxi's villages numbers 1 through 12. Now the Greater Huaxi (da huaxi) occupies an area of 30 square kilometers (about 7,400 acres), larger than Macau, and has a population of more than 30,000 (Tables 3.1 and 3.2).

Mr. Qü told me that it was the neighboring villages that approached Huaxi and asked to be merged. Each village that wanted to join Huaxi had to provide the approval signature from each villager. Huaxi would not accept the village unless all of its villagers agreed to the merger. It describes its way of merging as "one separation and five uniformities" (yifen wutong): the separation of village administration and corporate management, a unified management of the economy, the joint appointment of cadres, the combined

Table 3.1. *Huaxi Village population statistics, 2005*

|  | Population | | | Labor | | |
|---|---|---|---|---|---|---|
|  | Males | Females | Total | Village labor | Migrant workers | Emigrant workers |
| Huaxi Village | 861 | 847 | 1,708 | 1,551 | 14,246 | – |
| Huaxi No. 1 Village | 2,141 | 2,142 | 4,283 | 2,299 | 723 | 25 |
| Huaxi No. 2 Village | 1,795 | 1,787 | 3,582 | 2,050 | 450 | 50 |
| Huaxi No. 3 Village[a] | 1,537 | 1,476 | 3,013 | 2,058 | 7,200 | 10 |
| Huaxi No. 4 Village | 895 | 867 | 1,762 | 1,003 | 51 | 10 |
| Huaxi No. 5 Village | 1,342 | 1,270 | 2,612 | 1,507 | 740 | 15 |
| Huaxi No. 6 Village | 1,229 | 1,166 | 2,395 | 1,274 | 150 | 45 |
| Huaxi No. 7 Village | 1,111 | 1,104 | 2,215 | 1,040 | 100 | 20 |
| Huaxi No. 8 Village | 1,418 | 1,339 | 2,757 | 1,650 | 300 | – |
| Huaxi No. 9 Village | 955 | 866 | 1,821 | 900 | 50 | 20 |
| Huaxi No. 11 Village | 1,459 | 1,481 | 2,940 | 1,806 | 628 | 100 |
| Huaxi No. 12 Village | 1,038 | 1,037 | 2,075 | 1,127 | 200 | 30 |
| Total | 15,781 | 15,382 | 31,163 | 18,265 | 24,838 | 325 |

[a] Huaxi No. 3 Village is the former Jingbang Village. Before the merger, it emulated Huaxi's path of development and used to have a strong collective economy. However, because of ineffective management, many of the enterprises failed, and the villagers wanted to cash out. Huaxi offered the village 30 million yuan to settle with its members. As a result, people also call this village the "Money-assisted Village" (*Jinbang cun*).
Source: *Jiangyin Statistical Yearbook 2006*. Huaxi's No. 10 Village, Caihua Village, was not officially merged with Huaxi until September 3, 2006, so it is not included in the table.

job placement for qualified labor, a unified distribution of welfare benefits, and a coordinated plan for village construction. Therefore, except for the management of the villagers' daily lives (the village head would be elected by villagers in each village separately), the power to make all the important decisions about economic development was concentrated in Huaxi's original leadership, although several cadres from the villages being merged were also included in the core leadership of Greater Huaxi as deputy party secretaries.[8]

After the merger, the northern part of Huaxi was planned as the "granary" (*liangcang*), that is, the agricultural base that focuses on the development of new agricultural techniques and produce; the southern part was the "vault"

---

[8] Among the twenty-six Greater Huaxi party secretary and deputy party secretaries elected in 2003, two were from the merged villages. In the most recent election in January 2010, among the forty-one party secretaries, four were party secretaries of the merged villages.

Table 3.2. *Huaxi Village major economic statistics, 2005*

| | Industrial output (1,000 yuan) | Collective assets (1,000 yuan) | Collective debt (1,000 yuan) | Average income (per capita, yuan) |
|---|---|---|---|---|
| Huaxi Village | 24,517,670 | 4,829600 | 51,940 | 35,002 |
| Huaxi No. 1 Village | 249,030 | 14,580 | 60 | 10,892 |
| Huaxi No. 2 Village | 198,150 | 4,300 | – | 10,915 |
| Huaxi No. 3 Village | 61,100 | 9,880 | 2,540 | 10,878 |
| Huaxi No. 4 Village | – | 2,380 | 20 | 8,032 |
| Huaxi No. 5 Village | 91,970 | 4,260 | 20 | 10,310 |
| Huaxi No. 6 Village | 88,210 | 2,830 | 170 | 7,978 |
| Huaxi No. 7 Village | 8,100 | 810 | 160 | 7,600 |
| Huaxi No. 8 Village | 19,800 | 890 | 360 | 7,986 |
| Huaxi No. 9 Village | 97,720 | 2,400 | 60 | 7,717 |
| Huaxi No. 11 Village | 126,000 | 6,470 | – | 9,301 |
| Huaxi No. 12 Village | 38,000 | 1,750 | 480 | 8,405 |
| Total | 25,495,750 | 4,880,150 | 55,810 | 11,251* |

* This is the average income of Huaxi Village after the merger.
Source: *Jiangyin Statistical Yearbook 2006*. Huaxi's No. 10 Village, Caihua Village, was not officially merged with Huaxi until September 3, 2006, so it is not included in the table.

(*qianzhuang*), that is, the industrial district that includes Huaxi's No. 3 to 5 villages; and the central part was the "heaven" (*tiantang*), that is, the housing district which covers the original Huaxi, and the No. 1 and No. 2 villages.

## Socialism, Huaxi-Style

Like Nanjie, Huaxi's wealth results from the intelligent leadership, especially the party secretary whose charisma binds people together, the villagers' hard work, and its distinct way of organization and distribution. Go back to the quotation at the beginning of this chapter: "The sky of Huaxi is the sky of the Communist Party, the land of Huaxi is the land of socialism," written by Wu Renbao. To what extent can this highly industrialized and centralized village genuinely be called socialist or communist?

### The Dominant Leader: A Patriarchal System of Management

A highly capable party secretary seems to be a key factor in every successful collective model, but it is rare that anyone has the authority that Wu Renbao possessed. He was the star, in the same manner as Chen Yonggui in Dazhai, Yu Zuomin in Daqiuzhuang, and Shi Laihe in Liuzhuang. Those people have created the heroic stories of leading the villagers toward the transformation of their lives and also encouraging many others to follow the same example. They could probably become equally successful as private entrepreneurs, but they choose to be the "patriarch" of the village. All of them, except for Wu Renbao, are now dead. He seems to possess all three forms of authority that Weber categorized: charismatic, traditional, and legal-rational.

According to the Chinese administrative structure, the party secretary is supposed to have the most power, as the CCP guides the state. As a result, the authority of the party secretary has been institutionalized. However, not all party secretaries at the same administrative level have equal authority. Wu's authority also depends on his own charisma and long-established tradition. He has won people's respect and trust through his years of hard work and almost flawless leadership, making the right decisions at the right time, shouldering the responsibility of each difficult task, caring about the villagers' lives, and bringing about substantial economic achievements for Huaxi. People call him the "senior party secretary" (*lao shuji*) to distinguish him from the "new party secretary" (*xin shuji*), referring to Wu's youngest son, who was elected to the post in 2003. That title also indicates Wu's irreplaceable position in the villagers' mind, for he has been the dominant figure in this area for almost half a century. He works incredibly long hours, usually more than thirteen hours a day, and gets up at the crack of dawn to inspect the factories. He never uses an office but always works on site. In my interviews, several people complained about Huaxi's lack of vacation time, but they also said that many people felt ashamed to take a day off, because the senior party secretary in his late seventies never stops working.

Wu follows his own principles of The Three Prohibitions: do not take the best house in the village – in fact, he still resides in an old two-story house where he and his wife have lived for almost 30 years, while many young villagers or migrants have moved into the large, modern, European-style houses; do not take the highest salary; do not receive the largest bonus – he has given up more than 50 million yuan awarded to him by the upper-level administrations and left the money with the collective. He has a famous saying, "Even if one has tons of gold, one can only have three meals a day; no matter how luxurious a house one has, a person can only sleep in one bed" – a philosophy not too different from Buddhist doctrines. Throughout the village his slogans are hung everywhere. Visitors from all over the country, and even abroad, come to Huaxi, not just to see the village but also to meet him and listen to his speeches. The same holds true with the cadres from different administrative levels. He has become an icon inseparably linked to Huaxi.

His authority can even be mystified into some kind of divine power, as villagers claim that it never rains when Wu holds a village meeting and explain how some misfortunes often happen when he is not in the village. One such story is as follows. The rural fair day of a neighboring village was March 15 of the lunar calendar, and as it had rained every time on that day for many years, the village's party secretary changed its fair to another day, and Wu took over March 15 for Huaxi's fair. After the switch, it did not rain at all on the March 15, whereas the neighboring village still suffered from a wet fair despite the new date. People who understand probability know that those are two unrelated events, but it is coincidences like these that have enhanced Wu's authority in the villagers' mind, especially when they compare themselves to the neighboring village.

The legitimacy of his leadership is also based on his ability as a politician. He has hardly made any wrong decisions on major issues because he keeps a close eye on the changes in government policies and market conditions. "Seeking the truth from facts" (*shishi qiu shi*) is what appears repeatedly in the media when promoting the Huaxi model. As a result of this strategy, he decided not to divide the land in the late 1970s, as Huaxi had very little land per capita and a good industrial foundation. Instead, he contracted out the farmland to thirty people who were good at farming. For the same reason, he decided not to privatize the village enterprises in the early 1990s, but to allow for the coexistence of private and collective enterprises; what he calls "one village, two systems." However, he further stipulated that there should not be "one household, two systems" or "one person, two systems" for village cadres, because if in a family, the husband is the cadre, and the wife opens her own restaurant, then when the husband receives guests from elsewhere, it is very likely that he will take the guests to have meals at his wife's restaurant and charge the collective account for the costs. Such a rule minimized conflicts of interest and reduced corruption.

Wu Renbao summarizes his success at being a village party secretary into two principles: one is to be consistent (*baochi yizhi*) with the Party Central Committee (*dang zhongyang*) and thus with all the other levels of the administration,[9] and the other is to keep in touch with the masses (the villagers) and thus with all the Chinese people from different nationalities. Clearly, he views grassroots cadres as a bridge between the central

---

[9] Notice that here Wu emphasizes his consistence with the Central Committee, not the other levels of administration. For him, being consistent with the Central Committee means being consistent with all the other levels of governments.

government and the local people. However, it needs a lot of skill and courage when the interests of the two are not always the same.

In a review of Wu's authority, it is probably more understandable why the villagers did not make a fuss over the succession of Wu's youngest son as the new party secretary as many outsiders did. In Huaxi's leadership team consisting of one party secretary and twenty-four deputy party secretaries elected in 2003, fourteen were Wu's relatives (Table 3.3) and his oldest son Xiedong, second oldest son Xiede, youngest son Xie'en, daughter Yunfang, and son-in-law Miao Hongda have been in charge of the most profitable enterprises in Huaxi. In his speech at the Village Party Congress in 2003, Wu Renbao reported that Xiede contributed 42.8 percent of the available funds in Huaxi; Xie'en, 19.7 percent; Hongda, 18.6 percent; and Xiedong, 9.6 percent. The four of them thus controlled 90.7 percent of the village's total capital.[10] In the latest election in 2010, the core leadership increased to forty-one members. Although a few from the 2003 administration were not reelected as deputy party secretaries in 2010, more of Wu's relatives were on board in addition to the fourteen people elected in 2003, including one of Wu's daughters-in-law Sun Huifen, granddaughter Miao Hua, and grandson-in-law Lü Sujun. Wu's granddaughter-in-law, Zhou Li, became the number 2 figure in the ranking, only after Wu Xie'en, the party secretary.[11] Apparently, some of the third generation in the family became old enough to share power. In a word, almost every adult in the Wu family has been placed to the top of the power structure, and the core leadership of the village and village enterprises lies in the Wus.

Wu Renbao does not think that it creates any problem, although most outsiders would look at it as nepotism. For Wu, his twenty-six direct family members work for Huaxi rather than anywhere else, and that means they make a major contribution to the village's development and sacrifice their self-interest for the collective benefit. He does not think that his family members have been given any privileges but believes that all of them have risen to their current positions because of their own hard work and abilities.

However, given his authority in the village, it is natural to infer that his family members can get more opportunities, not necessarily outright material benefits or honor. For example, Wu Xie'en was sent by Wu Renbao

---

[10] See the report in *Beijing Youth Daily (Beijing Qingnian Bao)*, July 17, 2003, reproduced at http://www.people.com.cn/BIG5/jingji/1045/1972008.html.

[11] Source: Huaxi internal material, January 2010, provided by the Office of Propaganda.

Table 3.3. *Huaxi Party Secretary and Deputy Party Secretaries (Result of the 2003 Election)*

| Name | Sex | Education | Age | Position | Relation to Wu Renbao | Reelected in 2010? |
|---|---|---|---|---|---|---|
| Wu Xie'en* | M | High School | 39 | Party Secretary | 4th son (youngest) | Yes |
| Wu Renbao* | M | Associate College | 76 | Secretary of the General Office | Self | Yes |
| Wu Xiedong* | M | Associate College | 54 | Executive Party Secretary | Oldest son | Yes |
| Wu Xiede* | M | High School | 51 | Deputy Party Secretary (DPS) | 2nd son | Yes |
| Miao Hongda* | M | Associate High School | 47 | DPS | Son-in-law | Yes |
| Sun Yunnan* | M | College | 30 | DPS | Grandson-in-law | Yes |
| Bao Lijun* | F | Graduate School | 39 | DPS | Niece-in-law | Yes |
| Zhao Hefen* | F | High School | 51 | DPS | Maternal relative | Yes |
| Chen Xianmin* | M | College | 54 | DPS | University lecturer before coming to Huaxi in 1988 from Xi'an | No |
| He Jiannan* | M | Associate College | 39 | DPS | Maternal relative | Yes |
| Qu Jianjun* | M | Associate College | 35 | DPS | Born in Huaxi | Yes |
| Wu Yunfang | F | High School | 48 | DPS | Merge into Huaxi | No |
| Sun Dalong | M | High School | 51 | DPS | Merge into Huaxi | No |
| Qu Quanxing | M | High School | 37 | DPS | Born in Huaxi | Yes |
| Zhao Zhichu | M | Junior High | 49 | DPS | Cousin | Yes |
| Wu Fengying | F | Junior High | 47 | DPS | Daughter | Yes |
| Li Manliang | M | High School | 38 | DPS | Nephew | Yes |
| Li Jianjun | M | High School | 46 | DPS | Born in Huaxi | No |
| Tao Kuizhong | M | High School | 34 | DPS | Nephew-in-law | Yes |
| Yang Hongyu | F | Associate College | 34 | DPS | Maternal relative | Yes |
| Sun Haiyan | M | College | 29 | DPS | Came from Yancheng, Jiangsu in 1992 | Yes |
| Huang Jiangang | M | Associate College | 38 | DPS | From Huashi county where Huaxi is located | Yes |
| Yang Yongchang | M | Associate College | 39 | DPS | Came to Huaxi in 1997 as a private entrepreneur; joined the collective in 2002 | Yes |
| Zhou Dong | M | Associate College | 38 | DPS | Merge into Huaxi | No |
| Li Qing | M | College | 30 | DPS | Grandson-in-law | Yes |
| Guo Ding'an | M | High School | 51 | DPS | Merge into Huaxi | No |

* Also in the previous leadership elected in 2000 as either party secretary or deputy party secretary.

*Source:* Jiangyin City Huashi County Huaxi Village Material, July 2003, unpublished; Name List of Party-Village-Corporate Cadres for Discussion, January 2010, unpublished.

to help develop a poor and remote village in Heilongjiang in northeastern China. His achievements in that village became his political capital. In
his report to recommend Wu Xie'en as the sole candidate for party secretary, Wu Renbao said that he hoped that votes could reveal a consensus to
demonstrate the quality (*suzhi*) of each party member, to show if they had
principles and a conscience. In the end, Wu Xie'en was elected by a unan-
imous vote, while Wu Renbao himself received no votes. Clearly, Wu had
made up his mind to retire from the party secretary position to give his
son a chance. In addition, most of his grandchildren have studied or are
currently studying abroad, building their credentials to be the new leaders of Huaxi. Sun Yunnan, his grandson-in-law, studied in Japan and came
back to take charge of foreign trade and the textile industry and is now
both deputy party secretary and president of the Huaxi Group Corporation,
Ltd. listed on the Shenzhen Stock Exchange. Zhou Li, who studied in New
Zealand, now leads Huaxi's travel services. Wu Xieping's daughter studied
in Singapore and Germany and came back to Huaxi to work for her father
at the travel agency, and his son is still studying in Spain.

In celebration of the sixtieth anniversary of the founding of the People's
Republic of China in 2009, Huaxi built a Sixty-Year Memorial Hall to showcase the village's magnificent changes throughout all these years. On one
board, titled "A Devoted Family," a picture of Wu's three generations was
displayed. It seems that there is no intention for Wu to keep a low pro-
file concerning the concentration of power in his extended family. On the
other hand, Wu Xieping commented to me in 2010 that Huaxi's leadership
was democratically elected and that the current Party Committee contained
people with thirty-seven different surnames.

The expansion of the Party Committee in 2010 (with 41 party secretaries, 29 standing party committee members, and 35 members) definitely
means that more people are joining the decision-making process; however,
there is no doubt that Wu's family controls all the key political and economic positions to ensure that Huaxi does not deviate from the collectivist
path set by its charismatic leader. In fact, part of the reason why it was Wu's
youngest son rather than his other sons or daughter that succeeded as the
party secretary was because his age advantage that could ensure the continuity of the Huaxi model.[12] In this sense, the collective corporation has

---

[12] See the report in *Beijing Youth Daily (Beijing Qingnian Bao)*, July 17, 2003, reproduced at
http://www.people.com.cn/BIG5/jingji/1045/1972008.html. It was also confirmed in my
conversation with Wu Xieping: "My eldest brother is in charge of construction and real
estate, my second brother takes charge of trade, and my sister is responsible for logistics.

been restructured into a family business, not in terms of real ownership but in terms of actual operation. In a manner similar to the Lee Kuan Yew family in Singapore, members of the Wu family have invested themselves in the village and thus take ownership in the performance of the collective enterprises. From their point of view, they are not pocketing money into their personal account; instead, they are working for the prosperity of the collective, so their power is well justified. However, as in Nanjie or maybe in any system, coercion, including sanctions, peer pressure, and careful screening, is inevitable to keep the community ideologically homogenous and stable. Ms. Li, for example, a villager in the original Huaxi who now drives Huaxi's tourist cart, said that she was assigned to this job because she contradicted her superior and was later picked on and transferred from the trade company to her current job. Compared to her last job, driving tourist carts is more toilsome and has to endure exposure to sun and coldness. According to her, all the villagers in the original village have constant salaries but are assigned to jobs with different levels of intensity and work environments. Clearly, how close one is with the cadres can affect the job he or she gets.

Although Wu Renbao stepped down from the position of party secretary, he did not want to stay at home, so he created for himself a general office to supervise the cadres and to mediate public relations and is still considered to be the spiritual leader of the village. When I visited Huaxi in 2006, Wu claimed that he would retire at the age of 80. However, as I went back in 2010, Wu said in his speech at the village auditorium that he decided to postpone his retirement to 85. Because he was elected as a deputy to the National People's Congress at the age of 80 in 2007 and President Hu Jintao twice thanked him for his contribution to building the new socialist countryside, he felt encouraged to work for five more years.[13] It seems that unless he dies or loses his faculties, he will remain in power, no matter what the title is, because his legal-rational authority is supplemented by traditional patriarchal authority and charismatic authority. Such authority is strengthened by the support of the villagers, especially those in the original Huaxi, as a result of the creation of a common interest group, and stabilized through his family members and trusted people occupying important political and economic positions within the village.

My younger brother manages us all. He is young and can thus ensure a strong continuity" (Interview on June 24, 2010).

[13] Wu said in his speech that if President Hu only thanked him once, it might be out of courtesy; however, the fact that he said "thank you" twice meant that he was sincerely grateful. Those words were displayed in several tourist attractions in the village.

## The System of Distribution: Ability versus Needs

According to Huaxi's official sources, the poorest villager has 1 million yuan (about US$140,000) of savings and the richest does not exceed 10 million yuan (about US$1.4 million). Every family has a house, although with different square footages, and at least one car. Wu Renbao wants everyone in Huaxi to be rich, but not equally rich. As a result, the distribution system in Huaxi is unique. It is a mix of three forms: socialist distribution, based on one's labor input, with 20 percent of the bonus in cash, and the other 80 percent in the form of factory shares, similar to the employee stock options in the United States; communist distribution, based on one's need, with every villager enjoying welfare benefits worth at least 2,800 yuan per year[14]; and capitalist distribution linked to dividends – what Wu Renbao calls the kind of distribution found under the preliminary stage of socialism – which pays villagers dividends according to their ownership of village shares, usually at a rate of 5 percent[15] (Wu 2004).

To explain this system in more detail, before 2003, for each village factory, 20 percent of the profits could stay in the factory, and the remaining 80 percent was turned in to the corporate group. Now it is a 50/50 divide. For the amount of profits kept in the factory, 10 percent goes to the director, 30 percent is divided among other factory executives, another 30 percent is distributed to workers who are Huaxi villagers – 20 percent in cash and 80 percent as factory shares that can only accumulate dividends but can rarely get cashed out, and the remaining 30 percent stays as the fund for the factory's future development. In addition to the bonus linked to the profits of the factories, each villager also has a fixed bonus that is three times their base salary.

Villagers' dividend yield mainly comes from two sources: (1) dividends from the factory shares and other voluntary investments in the village enterprises at a fixed rate of 5 percent and (2) dividends from the village's forced fund-raising. Villagers have so far been asked to finance the village

---

[14] According to my interview with Mr. Li, a tourist guide in Huaxi's Travel Service Company whose dad bought a Huaxi *hukou*, Huaxi villagers receive 3,000 yuan a year as reimbursement for their utility bills and other expenses. Each person also gets 300 jin of rice every year at a price of 1 yuan per jin, which is much lower than the market price, and 5 kilograms of cooking oil. He said that all the daily expenses can be covered by the 3,000 yuan allowance. In my latest interview in 2010 with Mr. Wu, a retired deputy party secretary, villagers now also get free physical examinations for up to 5,000 yuan a year in expenses at the village's state-of-the-art health center, which cooperates with the Shanghai Changhai Hospital.

[15] According to my interviews in 2006, the rate was increased to 6%, although villagers could get up to 20%, and most would reinvest the money in the village corporation.

enterprises on three occasions: the first was in 1984 when all the village's adults were asked to each invest 2,000 yuan, and the dividends started to accumulate after 3 years at a fixed rate of 500 yuan a year; then, in 1998, the village's work force each invested 10,000 yuan, and in 2008, 30,000 yuan at an annual dividend rate of 8 to 20 percent.[16]

In sum, for villagers, as long as they work in the village enterprises, their rewards include the base salary (500–1,000 yuan), a bonus (three times the base salary plus a factory bonus), and an additional dividend of 5 percent or more for the capital villagers have invested. Retired villagers (females at the age of 50 and males at the age of 55) used to get pensions ranging from 7,700 to 13,600 yuan per year and all of their dining expenses and 90 percent of their health expenses were covered by the village. However, according to my latest interview in 2010, Huaxi has restructured its pay scheme since the new party secretary took power. Now, retirees in the Greater Huaxi receive 150 yuan per month in addition to rice and cooking oil, although the elderly in the original Huaxi can enjoy extra incomes coming from the dividends. The base salary for workers has increased to between 600 and 2,000 yuan depending on the nature of the job.

Huaxi's ideology promotes the idea that villagers should "talk more about accumulation, less about distribution; distribute less cash, and leave more for the transformation of the enterprises" (*shao fenpei, duo jilei, shao na xianjin duo rugu*). It is said that this idea comes from Wu Renbao who dislikes owing debt or overspending. Therefore, how much to be distributed for personal disposal and how much to be put into village production is constrained by the decisions of the leadership. Even though a person may have millions of yuan in his household savings account, he cannot freely take the money out, as the account is kept by the village. Each year only 1 percent of the dividends can actually be cashed out; the remaining part will be reinvested into the village enterprises and credited to the villager's personal account, although it is said that the new party secretary, Wu Xie'en, does not restrict villagers from withdrawing money as much as his father did and also encourages them to enjoy their lives. The young leader is also bolder in taking advantage of financial leverage and has expanded Huaxi's economy into real estates and financial services.

If one leaves the village, all the money in the account will be forfeited to the village; they call it repaying the debt owed to the collective. This manner of distribution serves at least two purposes: first, villagers are forced to stay and contribute to the village, because the stakes of leaving the collective are too

[16] Based on my interview with the retirees in Huaxi on June 25, 2010.

high; second, the village as a whole has a greater cash flow to expand existing projects and to develop new ones and does not have to be too dependent on external funds. This can be viewed as a collective financing process with each villager offering loans with an indefinite maturity to the community through the value of their labor input and cash contributions. Of course, it also provides villagers with a good source of investment with a high interest rate and almost no risks as the rate of return is more or less fixed.

This financing and distribution structure is different from Nanjie's, as personal investment is closely tied to the performance of village enterprises in Huaxi, whereas in Nanjie personal investment is limited to the funding at the outset of the village's industrialization. Subsequently, the launching of new projects depends largely on loans from the banks. Of course, Nanjie villagers get a fixed and low income, and the difference between the market price of their labor and the actual income they receive can also be regarded as their investment to sustain the public good. Overall, in both Nanjie and Huaxi villagers need to pay a "breakup fee" if they want to leave the "big family"; therefore, the more welfare benefits they enjoy, the more they are tied up in the collective economy.

Nonetheless, this distribution system is confined to the villagers in the original Huaxi, that is, the central village (*zhongxin cun*). For villages that have just been merged into Huaxi – members of the Greater Huaxi (*da huaxi*) – they do not have any village shares except for those given to them immediately after the merger,[17] or if they work in the factories, they can get factory shares. Very few of them have moved into the apartment buildings in Huaxi, and most of them still live in their old houses.[18] As for now, European-style villas seem to be a faraway dream for them. The good thing is that villagers in Greater Huaxi can be guaranteed a position in one of the many village enterprises, and their salaries, other things being equal, are higher than those of the migrant workers.

Li, a tourist guide in his early twenties, whose father bought Huaxi *hukou* and became a Huaxi villager,[19] told me that Huaxi villagers are divided into three strata (*san deng*): people in the highest stratum are those living in the

---

[17] For the villages that merged with Huaxi before 2003, each college graduate was given 50,000 shares, senior high school graduates 30,000 shares, and junior high school graduate 10,000 shares. There were no more shares for villages that became part of Huaxi in 2004.

[18] Based on interviews with the migrant workers whose relatives are members of the merged villages in March 2006.

[19] His father bought a Huaxi *hukou* in 2003. That was the only time that Huaxi *hukou* was openly sold to the public at a price of 10,000 yuan for college graduates and 30,000 yuan for people with high school diplomas, designed to attract talent to come and settle in Huaxi.

central village with village share dividends, welfare benefits, and big houses; the second stratum includes people who bought their *hukou* and talents who were granted Huaxi *hukou* because of their contribution to Huaxi, and many of them live in the apartment buildings, some in the villas; the lowest stratum comprises the villagers who merged into Huaxi. Lingling, another tourist guide in Huaxi whose parents have worked in the village for over 13 years, told me a similar story. She said

[People in] the central village have share subsidies. People in both the central village and the surrounding villages (*zhoubian cun*) are allocated 300 jin of rice, 15 jin of cooking oil, and free breakfasts and lunches at the dining halls. Anyway, in Huaxi villagers form one stratum, villagers of the merged villages form another, and the migrant workers form the lowest stratum.

In fact, there are also different strata within the central village. For example, although houses in the central village are collectively built and furnished, each household has to pay for them. Money is deducted from their account in the village according to the building cost of the houses, unrelated to the market price. However, having the money to buy does not guarantee that one will actually get the house one wants; it also depends on one's social status in the village, for example, whether all of the family members work in the village enterprises, how long they have been in the village, and how much they can contribute to the village at their positions. There are five kinds of houses built in different years: the best and most recently built type is European-style, single-family houses valued at 1.3 to 2.5 million yuan; the second to the fourth types are single-family houses with a similar square footage – usually 400 square meters (4,300 square feet) – but very different layouts and furnishings and thus cost differently; and the last type is two-story condo units with shared utilities (*tongzilou*) built in 1976, the type that Wu Renbao still lives in. Each block of houses are separately planned and located.

When I visited the village again in June 2010, several other housing communities were being constructed, some for the villagers and others for public sales. One notable construction was the supposedly eighth tallest building in China and fifteenth in the world, a 328-meter multipurpose building that combines a five-star hotel, conference facilities, dining services, and residential apartments (Figure 3.2). Obviously as land has become scarcer, Huaxi chose to develop vertically. The retirees in the village told me that approximately 200 households in the original Huaxi would move out of their current single-family houses and into this new construction after its completion, as they had all invested in its construction.

Figure 3.2. The 328-meter skyscraper under construction. Photo by the author.

What kind of house one lives in and how much money one has in the village account partly reflects a person's social status in the village. Most cadre and corporate executive families, except for Wu Renbao and his children, live in the most luxurious European-style houses. They are the wealthiest people in Huaxi who control the village's major decisions and economic operations. This, on the one hand, indicates that the most talented and capable people in the village are included in the elite circle, thus stabilizing the collective model, as less capable people would have an even lower chance of success if they leave the collective. On the other hand, this stratification can lead to conflict between ordinary villagers and the elite, as well as among the elite. Therefore, the patriarchal system and cultural and ideological reinforcement help mitigate the potential conflict.

The compensation of migrant workers is quite low, considering their working hours and lack of vacation time. Salaries vary, depending on the performance of the factory and the nature of the job. Factory workers' incomes usually consist of a base salary and piece rates. Those working in the factories get higher salaries than those in the travel service company serving as guides or hotel attendants. Technicians, salespeople, and others with special talents have a higher income than workers in the workshops.

However, none of them receives the communist and capitalist distribution that Huaxi villagers enjoy. To stabilize the workforce, only half of the salaries are given to the migrant workers every month, and the other half are provided in a lump sum at the end of each year. Bonuses are allocated during the following year. If a worker resigns, he will be given less salary and a reduced bonus. Workers usually start with a meager salary and receive pay raises for each additional year they serve.

Mr. Xue, for instance, who cleans floors for one of Huaxi's hotels, was only paid 300 yuan per month at first, while he paid 500 yuan to the village as a deposit, which has never been returned to him. As of 2010, he had a monthly salary of a little over 1,000 yuan. He works from 6 AM until the dining services in the hotel close, sometimes 8 PM, other times 10 PM, depending on when the guests leave, and does not have any days off. Nonetheless, all of his family members work in Huaxi, and he was happy that the whole family could be together. Although his elder daughter's child stays with the in-laws in Henan, as schools in Huaxi are too expensive for non-villagers like them and today salaries in the village are not as competitive as those in his hometown any more, he has no plans to leave yet as he thinks that he has gone through the most difficult time.

Nevertheless, the turnover rate is not low in Huaxi especially during the Spring Festival. Lingling told me that at this time of the year workers at the travel agency were given forty to sixty days off, depending on whether they were from Jiangsu, where Huaxi is located, or other provinces.[20] However, workers at the factory can hardly take a leave, and almost have no free weekends. As a scholar who has been studying Huaxi for a long time commented, the management at Huaxi, like many other shrewd southern businesspeople, can be stingy (*keke*) toward migrant workers at times. Some of the village's economic practices further evade national laws such as those guaranteeing vacations for workers, and the way it collects money from its villagers is similar to illegal fund-raising,[21] referring to the forced savings and financing of village enterprises.

Even though migrant workers take the least desirable jobs and get the lowest salaries, over 30,000 of them work in Huaxi each year. Li said that he

---

[20]   Interview on March 13, 2006.

[21]   Informal interview on March 12, 2006. The state has imposed several regulations to stop illegal fund-raising. However, there are no clear definitions of what illegal fund-raising is. The state forbids illegally taking deposits from the public or issuing stocks or corporate bonds without authorization. Nevertheless, because there are limited sources of investment for ordinary people and it is difficult for small- and mid-sized nonpublic enterprises to get financed, people often rely on unauthorized channels to get loans and credit.

wanted to stay in Huaxi to acquire skills and gain experience: "Huaxi won't fire you, because it is in critical need of labor." The same holds true with Lingling. She told me that there were advantages in being migrant workers, because they were allowed to operate private businesses to supplement their wages, unlike the villagers. She said she wanted to open a small store in Huaxi, but her parents said she was too young and needed more experience. They both agreed that the longer one stays in Huaxi, the higher the level of one's personal income and social status. This kind of labor policy is similar to Nanjie. Many young people who have just got out of school join those village enterprises for the purpose of getting experience, and they provide the village with cheap labor, creating an internship labor market. They choose those collectively owned enterprises partly because jobs are safe and stable, pay is more reliable, and the working environment is better than many private enterprises. Others like Mr. Xue stay because their children also work in the village, usually having better jobs and salaries than the older generation. In addition, although incomes in Huaxi are not as competitive as those in Shanghai or other big cities, living costs are also much lower, so they are still able to save money. Mrs. Li, also from Henan, who used to work in Shanghai and now washes dishes in one of Huaxi's hotels, told me that except for the rent and utilities, her family barely needs to spend any money, as meals are provided by the hotel.[22]

It is very hard for migrant workers to mix with the villagers, although they may interact with them at work. Only people with the village IDs or a special permit are allowed in the village's housing district. Visitors need to sign a form and leave their IDs with the guards before going inside the village, and that excludes the housing district where there is another checkpoint. Only when touring around with a guide from the village's travel service company is one allowed to enter the housing district, and the houses that can be visited are decided by the guide, or more accurately, predetermined by the village leaders. Such strict security measures are said to protect the villagers who are becoming increasingly wealthier. However, clearly they also set a boundary between villagers and non-villagers, both physically and mentally, and ensure that the village knows whoever enters their community.

In his classic volume on group boundaries, Fredrick Barth (1969) argues that ethnic groups do not need to live in isolation to maintain their boundaries, as group identities are the product of continuous ascription and self-ascription, meaning the interactional processes of inclusion and

---

[22] Interview on June 24, 2010.

exclusion. Therefore, by dichotomizing between members and outsiders, group boundaries are constantly maintained and reinforced, and groups can thus survive changing membership and participation. Any group or organization is faced with the question of balancing autonomy and control and between differentiation and integration. Although resorting to different norms and values, both Nanjie and Huaxi are organized around a charismatic leader whose authority has been routinized and who has managed to motivate and mobilize the villagers by creating a group boundary to differentiate itself from others. Villagers, more or less, take pride in their villages, or their groups. The different distribution systems among villagers and non-villagers also serve as a way to strengthen group boundaries and enhance internal integration. The job of maintaining cohesion is more complicated in Huaxi, as it extends its boundary to include sixteen other villages that have contributed their land to the village's industrial development yet are not fully sharing its prosperity as the original villagers are. How successful it can incorporate those new members depends on whether the common identity of being a Huaxi villager is fully ascribed and recognized.

In both Huaxi and Nanjie, by creating a two or more tiered distribution system, the original communal and cooperative village enterprises are turning into something similar to a traditional capitalist partnership, although with a large number of partners – the villagers – and a long arm that penetrates into the work and life of its members. Such an arrangement has been called "collective selfishness" (Gunn 2000), as the original members are unwilling to give up their privileges and share their profits with outsiders or new entrants. It strengthens the bond among existing members but, at the same time, sets the village apart from the prototypical cooperative.

### Culture and Ideology

Wu Renbao has another much quoted saying: "We need to enrich our head after enriching our pockets." In 1988, he established the Huaxi Cultural and Ethical Development Company (*Huaxi Jingshen Wenming Kaifa Gongsi*) in charge of different training sessions for peasants, workers, cadres, and even cadres from other places as well as the village's media coverage and public relations. It operates like an enterprise, with employees producing, distributing, and marketing intangible products such as knowledge, information, skills, and values that are supplemental to the village's economic production. Huaxi also has a Special Arts Troupe, under the leadership of Wu, to promote the Huaxi model and different village policies through theatrical performances. Similar to Nanjie, it understands the importance of cultural and social capital for a village based on collective ownership and distribution.

Some people argue that the Huaxi model is a system that is equivalent to Singapore.[23] As in both cases, tremendous economic growth is accompanied by a patriarchal system and an emphasis on the Confucian values of social hierarchy, obedience, sacrifice of individuality for the pursuit of collective interests, and strong work ethic. Though Confucianism is not the official ideology of Huaxi, one can still easily figure out the traces of Confucian values from the building of a pavilion depicting the twenty-four stories about filial piety (*ershisi xiao ting*), and the village's emphasis on family harmony and respect for the elderly. In Huaxi, once an elderly villager reaches 100 years old, the village will reward each member in the extended family with 10,000 yuan (US$1,400). In 2001, Mrs. Qü's family received 370,000 yuan in total as a reward.[24]

Unlike Nanjie that proposes an official ideology of Maoism, Huaxi demonstrates its flexibility. There are statues of Confucius, Lao Tzu, Buddha, Jesus, the Virgin Mary, and various legendary heroes from feudal China to communist China. The pagodas with golden tops, a blend of Buddhism and traditional Chinese folk religion, are Huaxi's hotels, apartments, and office buildings. Of course, they have also become tourist attractions for visitors from all over the country. Wu said that urbanization means to draw the urban dwellers to visit and spend money. With the growing tourist industry, the village is building itself into a rural theme park. Needless to say, a sound economy is crucial for sustaining the collective model. Therefore, whatever is good for the collective economy will be followed. In this sense, I think Huaxi's values consist of two parts: first, the pursuit of wealth, and second, the interdependence of the collective and individuals.

Like Nanjie, Huaxi also has many different kinds of meetings – a socialist tradition. Corporate executives and workers alike will attend meetings every day. The executives meet first before the workers are gathered to pass on important policies and information. For villagers, a briefing meeting is held every week to make sure that they are on the same page with the leadership. Of course, this also means that village leaders and elites control and filter information for the villagers, creating asymmetric power relations.

---

[23]  See, for example, Cheng Li, "Is a Rich Man Happier than a Free Man? Huaxi Village, China's 'Mini-Singapore,'" in *Rediscovering China: Dynamics and Dilemmas of Reform* (Lanham, MD: Rowman & Littlefield, 1997).

[24]  Mrs. Qü was the vice managing director of the Huaxi Travel Service Co., one of my interviewees in 2006.

To Wu, socialism means people's happiness, measured by a comfortable life, a light heart, and a healthy body; communism is when all mankind is happy. Nevertheless, he also seems to be a follower of Taylor's (1911) scientific management principles, which maintains that managers are the head of the organization and workers the hands, and that the head needs to tell the hands the best way of doing things. Therefore, villagers are not involved in the decision-making process as in real cooperatives, even though they are informed of the decisions and share the profits. The Huaxi model seems to be a microcosm of what China is currently undergoing on a larger scale, struggling with different forms of distribution and structures of ownership, but the crucial difference is that Huaxi has a sound economic foundation that many other areas lack. On the other hand, it demonstrates that a collective economy can be economically successful and, on occasions, even more effective than a private economy. However, instead of being a monolith, there are different strata and diverse values within the community. These are integrated by a unique distribution system that lays emphasis on being rich but not equally rich, a patriarchal system that stabilizes the collective model, and a group identity based on a sense of pride and achievement through common experiences in the village's history of uneven development.

Like Nanjie, Huaxi is also restructuring its economy, albeit a step ahead of Nanjie. It is moving away from traditional manufacturing that dominated Wu Renbao's times to services and green technologies, something initiated by Wu Xie'en as the new generation of leader. The exploration continues.

# FOUR

# Capitalism Reborn or Collectivism Rediscovered?

By three methods we may learn wisdom: First, by reflection, which is noblest; Second, by imitation, which is easiest; and third by experience, which is the bitterest.
Confucius, *The Analects of Confucius* (400 BC)

DiMaggio and Powell (1983) have argued that organizations, in face of uncertainty and constraint, often resemble each other in structures and practices to gain legitimacy rather than improved performance or efficiency – what they call "institutional isomorphism." Such a synchronizing process may be a result of political constraint, social pressure, professional prescriptions such as recommendations made by consultants, or inter-organizational networks. In rural China, although a certain level of diffusion and imitation may exist, hence the discussion of models, local variations and innovations abound, often out of bitter experience. After all, when the whole state is "crossing the river by touching the stones" (*mozhe shitou guohe*), which creates an extreme scenario of uncertainty but also opportunity and flexibility, concerns about legitimacy are second to unleashing human creativity or improvising coping strategies. If Nanjie and Huaxi support the "trickle down" effect – to borrow a term from the economists – where villagers benefit from a strong, centralized collective economy, Shangyuan Village tells the opposite story of the "spreading branch" effect, where the collective thrives through numerous successful private businesses.

Located in Wenzhou city, Zhejiang province, the prototype of China's private economy, Shangyuan is one of China's Ten Most Affluent Villages (*zhongguo shijia xiaokang cun*) (Map 4.1). However, it is not as widely covered by the media as Huaxi or Nanjie in the latest campaign of "building a new socialist countryside," being less controversial than the other two rural models in transitional China. Nor does it have neat and wide streets or carefully planned rows of villas similar to American suburbia. It looks more

Map 4.1. Location of Shangyuan Village.

like a small and bustling urban community. Situated in the center of Liushi town, the base of the production and distribution of low-voltage electrical equipment in China, the village is barely distinguishable from the town. There is hardly any arable farmland left in the village, and in fact, when I visited it in 2006, the average price of housing rose to over 8,000 yuan per square meter (roughly US$100 per square foot) – close to, if not higher than, that in many Chinese cities.

## Wenzhou and the Private Economy

### Developing a Private Economy in China

Since 1978, market-oriented economic reform in China has led to significant changes in social relations and new alignments of interests. Complete reliance on state-owned and collective enterprises has been replaced by a mixed economy, where the private sector plays an increasingly important role in the national economy. Private enterprises (*siying qiye*) have not only contributed to the fast economic growth of China but also provide thousands of employment opportunities to the society, which can mitigate the social costs of the reform of state-owned enterprises (SOE) and the financial sector. Between 1991 and 2000 – the first decade of the development of the private economy in China before its entry into the World Trade Organization – the number of domestic private firms and their employees both grew on an average of more than 30 percent a year, and the value of industrial output increased at an average rate of almost 67 percent annually (Table 4.1, Figure 4.1). As indicated by the official statistics, by the end of 2004, more than 96 million people were either employed in the private enterprises or self-employed, nearly 13 percent of the total employed population.[1]

China's approach to market-oriented reforms is characterized by its extensive local experimentation and a "dual track" strategy. The so-called dual track system was first used in price reform and later introduced to other structural changes including a shift in ownership. It refers to the adoption of some elements of a market economy while operating under the old regimen of a planned economy in hope of possibly reducing the costs of the intense political conflict or turmoil experienced by countries such as the former Soviet Union. This dual tracking greatly influenced the development of the private sector in China.

Private enterprises first occurred in the rural areas with the implementation of the household responsibility system between 1978 and 1982. As collective agricultural production ended, surplus rural laborers were liberated to engage in market-oriented rural industries, such as the TVEs, and some started their own small businesses. However, for the first approved private

---

[1]   *China Statistical Yearbook 2005* at http://www.stats.gov.cn/tjsj/ndsj/2005/indexeh.htm.

Table 4.1. *Development of private enterprises in China, 1991–2000*

| Year | Firms | | Employment* | | Industrial output** | |
|---|---|---|---|---|---|---|
| | Number (thousands) | Growth (%) | Number (thousands) | Growth (%) | Value (billions of yuan) | Growth (%) |
| 1991 | 107.8 | | 1,839 | | 14.7 | |
| 1992 | 139.6 | 29.5 | 2,318 | 26.1 | 20.5 | 39.5 |
| 1993 | 237.9 | 70.4 | 3,726 | 60.7 | 42.2 | 105.9 |
| 1994 | 432.2 | 81.7 | 6,480 | 73.9 | 115.4 | 173.5 |
| 1995 | 654.5 | 51.4 | 9,560 | 47.5 | 229.5 | 98.9 |
| 1996 | 819.3 | 25.2 | 11,710 | 22.5 | 322.7 | 40.6 |
| 1997 | 960.7 | 17.3 | 13,500 | 15.3 | 392.3 | 21.6 |
| 1998 | 1,201 | 25.0 | 17,100 | 26.7 | 585.3 | 49.2 |
| 1999 | 1,509 | 25.6 | 20,220 | 18.2 | 768.6 | 31.3 |
| 2000 | 1,762 | 16.8 | 24,070 | 19.0 | 1,074.0 | 39.7 |
| Average | | 38.1 | | 34.4 | | 66.7 |

* Data of employment only include those in the category of private enterprises in both urban and rural China, not self-employment, joint ventures, foreign-owned companies, or other types of non-state-owned businesses.
** Output values are calculated in 1989 constant prices.
*Source*: China Industrial and Commerce Administrative Management Yearbook, 1992–2000; China Statistical Yearbook, 1992–2001.

businesses – that is, individual enterprises (*geti qiye*) – regulations limited the number of employees to a maximum of seven and stipulated that these enterprises could only be owned by farmers, retirees, or unemployed persons. Larger private businesses, called private enterprises (*siying qiye*), were not officially recognized until 1988, as these individual enterprises developed and expanded (Pearson 1997). During the 1980s and early 1990s, the Party and the state wavered on whether they should encourage the growth of the private sector, particularly the involvement of party members in private businesses.

Because of uncertain government policies, many private entrepreneurs were worried about their rights and the security of their property. Development of the private sector was thus largely restricted and many private enterprises became "red hat" collectives – enterprises that were privately owned and operated but were registered as collectively owned in order to gain official sanction and protection (Nee 1992; Pearson 1997; Dickson 2003). Such a phenomenon was quite prevalent in the two decades of reform before the turn of the century. According to a sample survey carried out by the State Administration for Industry and Commerce in 1994, 83 percent of the registered TVEs were actually privately owned. Some

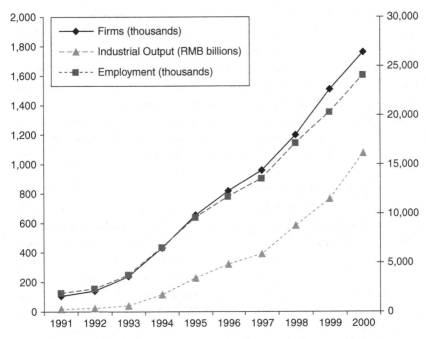

Figure 4.1. Trend of private enterprise development in China, 1991-2000.

private entrepreneurs even got involved in corruption scandals, as they offered bribes to government officials to gain preferences. Local cadres also took advantage of the politically vulnerable private enterprises, asking for all kinds of "management fees" and donations. In return, they were provided with information or some of the advantages enjoyed only by the SOEs, such as favorable land, tax, and loan policies. Meanwhile, despite the preferences, productivity and profits in SOEs continued to plunge, whereas private enterprises were able to sustain fast growth. Consequently, there was a need for better-defined property rights and ownership and for the legitimation of the economic position of private enterprises (Nee 1992).

In the 1990s, especially toward the end of the decade, government and party policies attached increasing importance to shifting to a market economy and ruling the country by law rather than by networks (*guanxi*) or the commands of officials. Meanwhile, further opening to the outside world resulted in an increase in foreign direct investment in China, which gave further impetus to the development of the private sector. In 1997, at the 15th National Party Congress of the CCP, the then President Jiang Zemin declared that the nonpublic enterprises were "an important component part of the socialist market economy."[2] This was later written into the 1999 Amendment to the Constitution to change the original description of the nonpublic economy as "a complement to the state-owned economy."[3] In 2002, during the 16th National Party Congress, Jiang in his political report referred to executives and managers in non-state sectors and self-employed laborers as the "builders of socialism with Chinese characteristics."[4] He further stated that all legitimate income, whether from labor or non-labor, should be protected. This clarified the social status and property rights of people working in the private sector. In November 2002, China's first Civil Code was submitted to the National People's Congress, and it included several articles to protect personal assets and the property of private enterprises (Li 2003). On March 16, 2007, the Congress passed a property rights law, which, for the first time since 1949, offered legal protection to private property, including the means of production like factories and workshops, although agricultural land remains collectively owned, and the current 30-year leasing term to the peasants was untouched by the law.

There are various accounts of the emergence and development of a private economy in China as discussed in the first chapter: the market transition theory, the clientelist ties between local governments and private entrepreneurs, and the revival of family and pseudo-family ties. The three models capture different aspects of the private sector in China. It does not necessarily mean that the market mechanism, clientelist ties, and family and kinship ties cannot coexist in transitional China. In fact, the development of a private economy in Wenzhou clearly demonstrates the mobilization of all three elements.

### The Wenzhou Model
Wenzhou prefecture, situated in southeastern Zhejiang, is renowned for its thriving private economy, and people there are often referred to as the "Jews

2  For an English version of the full text of Jiang Zemin's speech at the 15th Party Congress entitled "Hold High the Great Banner of Deng Xiaoping Theory for an All-round Advancement of the Cause of Building Socialism with Chinese Characteristics to the 21st Century," see http://www.fas.org/news/china/1997/970912-prc.htm. The Chinese version can be found at http://news.xinhuanet.com/ziliao/2003–01/20/content_697189.htm.
3  It is in Article 16 of the Amendment to revise Article 11 in the Constitution. For an English version of the Amendment, see http://www.china.org.cn/china/LegislationsForm2001–2010/2011–02/12/content_21907042.htm.
4  For an English version of the full text of Jiang Zemin's speech at the 16th Party Congress entitled "Building a Well-off Society in an All-Round Way and Creating a New Situation in Building Socialism with Chinese Characteristics," see http://english.peopledaily.com.cn/200211/18/eng20021118_106983.shtml. The Chinese version can be found at http://news.xinhuanet.com/ziliao/2002–11/17/content_693542.htm.

of China" for their sharp business acumen. People in Wenzhou started their private businesses, often secretively but with the local governments' acquiescence, long before the reforms took place nationally. Set up in 1986, the prefecture was the first "special experimental zone for the development of the commodity economy" in the reform era.

Wenzhou, with a population of more than 7.8 million, is the most heavily populated city in Zhejiang. It was historically separated from the rest of the province by its rugged terrain and distinct dialect. Unlike northern Zhejiang which is known as the land of rice and fish (*yumi zhixiang*) and greatly influenced by its proximity to Shanghai, Wenzhou was mountainous, populous yet short of resources, and often described as "seventy percent mountains, twenty percent water, and ten percent farmland" (*qishan ershui yifen tian*).[5] Agriculture was unlikely to prosper because of the scarcity and low quality of farmland. For a long time, waterways were the only access to other regions of China. The ecological and geographical conditions made life there more difficult than other parts of Zhejiang. Moreover, the distinctive dialect also isolated Wenzhou, as it is very different not only from Mandarin, the standard Chinese conversational language, but also from other dialects in Zhejiang. According to a 1955 report, the Wenzhou dialect was understood only within a 34-mile radius of the city's radio station (Parris 1993).

In addition, because it borders Fujian province to the south and is directly across the Straits from Taiwan, Wenzhou received little state investment, since it was perceived as a strategically vulnerable front line against Taiwan and any input might be reduced to ruins if a war broke out (Map 4.2). Between 1949 and 1981, the total state investment in Wenzhou was merely 655 million yuan, whereas Ningbo, another port city in Zhejiang, received 2.8 billion yuan (Parris 1993).

As a Chinese maxim indicates, "poverty gives rise to a desire for change (*qiong ze si bian*)." When asked why Wenzhou is the way it is now, many of my interviewees said that it was all because of poverty. Unfavorable natural conditions and insufficient state aid left people with no other choice but to find alternative strategies to survive. They started up household workshops to supplement agriculture even before the central government lifted the ban on the private economy. Many also migrated to other parts of China or Southeast Asia or Europe as vendors or small-business owners. In fact, there are so many people from Wenzhou involved in business in Rome that it was a frequent joke among my respondents that even the Italian police have

---

[5]   This description was frequently referred to by my interviewees.

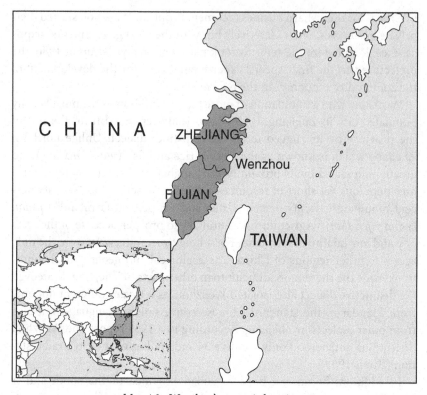

Map 4.2. Wenzhou's strategic location.

to learn the Wenzhou dialect.[6] Self-reliance is deeply rooted in the culture of Wenzhou, and many observers claim that the success of the Wenzhou model is a result of the local people's hard work and intelligence instead of state or foreign investment. Wenzhou built its own railway, airport, and university without any state funding. Many of the interviewees told me that there was no word for "laid-off workers" (*xiagang zhigong*) in their dictionary. When individuals from other parts of China were complaining about the huge waves of layoffs in the SOEs as a result of the economic restructuring, people in Wenzhou were working to expand their own businesses, as there has hardly been any SOE in Wenzhou for the last three decades.

Even though many articles have been written about Wenzhou, it is hard to tell what exactly a "Wenzhou model" is, except for its many household or private businesses. It piqued my interest when a relative of a friend of

---

[6]  Interview with the Sun family in the city of Wenzhou in 2006.

mine, who owns a sewing machine factory in Wenzhou, commented that the essence of the Wenzhou model was its people's boldness, and "boldness" was thereafter reiterated by several of my interviewees. It is said that people in Wenzhou are not afraid of any undertakings, even illegal or life-threatening ones, as long as there are profits. As a result, you see Wenzhou business people in Iraq, remote parts of Africa, and North Korea. Sun Yi, in his late twenties, an owner of an interior design company in Wenzhou, told me,

I know a friend who went to Jiamusi [a city in Northeastern China near the border with Russia], and invested money to build the best department store in the city, selling products made in Wenzhou or other parts of Zhejiang. He has been there for several decades, and so has his family. Life is very harsh in Jiamusi. Who really wants to be so far away from home and live such an unsettled life? But that's how Wenzhou people survive. People at that time were very poor, and thus have developed stamina and a daring character. I have a client, who drives a small Suzuki and wears muddy shoes and very ordinary clothes, but he actually owns a big factory.

In a word, where there is a business opportunity, there go Wenzhou people.

When Wenzhou products were first on the national market in the 1980s, they were hailed for their cheap prices and fashionable designs – often copying the most popular brands on the market. However, products made in houschold workshops with shabby tools and poor working conditions were doomed to be of low quality. Although seizing the good timing of reform and an emerging consumer market, Wenzhou people were soon denounced for their shoddy products. In 1987 a well-known incident occurred in Hangzhou, capital of Zhejiang, in which more than 5,000 made-in-Wenzhou shoes were burnt by angry consumers. In an interview, Hong Zhenning, vice chair of the Wenzhou Social Science Association, calls this first stage of primitive accumulation in Wenzhou's economic development the "competition of quantity" (*shuliang jingzheng*). The well-known Qiaotou button market in Yongjia County started with people selling usable buttons found in trash. There were also cases of peddling fake government seals and business invoices, as private enterprises used to have a difficult time getting access to them. For a long time after, the Wenzhou model lost its appeal, as people regarded it as unethical.

However, entering the 1990s, after the initial phase of capital accumulation, entrepreneurs in Wenzhou began to pay attention to the quality and brand image of their products. They hired research and development, marketing, and sales specialists to help build up their own brands. Since 1991, a trade fair of well-known, high-quality Wenzhou products has been held in Beijing annually. The press, state leaders, and celebrities are invited to boost the overall image of Wenzhou products. Now Wenzhou boasts over forty national-level famous brands and is ranked as one of the top five cities manufacturing these prestigious products. From street vendors to business owners with factories and sales networks, the smugglers and profiteers have transformed themselves into entrepreneurs. Qiaotou, as previously mentioned, has also become the nation's largest button market, producing for people all over the world.

As is the case for many businesses in Hong Kong and Southeast Asia, family and kinship ties are crucial in expanding household workshops into large private businesses. When it was almost impossible for private ventures to get loans from state-run banks, entrepreneurs in Wenzhou managed to mobilize private capital through their networks, including traditional, self-organized credit associations and private loans arranged directly or through a middle man who would receive a fee. This kind of credit was based more on trust and reputation than on contracts. In addition, private banks and credit unions were established to fund nonpublic enterprises from as early as the 1980s. Also, because of the initial small scale of household businesses, businesspeople are good at grouping together to strike a better and bigger deal from which everybody can benefit. For example, when an order of eyeglasses arrives, the firm that gets the order will inform other related enterprises, such as the ones making the frames, lenses, eyeglass cases, and cleaning cloths, respectively, and they will together complete the order, reducing costs and benefiting from economies of scale through neither market nor hierarchy but the network forms of organization.

Therefore, when a business opportunity comes, unlike other places where businesses are most likely to have an internecine fight (*wolidou*) for a piece of the "cake," people in Wenzhou work on making the cake bigger. A "cluster economy" is thus developed; businesses in related industries or product lines are often located close to each other and form loosely coupled networks. In Wenzhou, several clusters have been established, such as the printing industry in Cangnan County, the valve industry in Ouhai District, the pen producing industry in Longwan District, the low-voltage electrical equipment industry in Yueqing County, and the shoe, garment, and cigarette lighter industries in the city of Wenzhou.

The Wenzhou model certainly means flexibility. People will make whatever products are profitable on the market, and they are also good at exploring market information. When other Chinese were being happily employed by foreign bosses, many in Wenzhou learned from foreign investors and set up factories in other parts of China to take advantage of the low labor cost, abundant land, and cheap raw materials. When others still regarded housing as a social welfare benefit and a necessity for life, people in Wenzhou started to buy and sell houses for profits, directly driving the real estate prices in many big cities to record high levels. After the housing market, they started to become involved in the coal market and, more recently, the speculation on agricultural produce. It seems that they can always find "structural holes" in the system. Some blame people in Wenzhou for disrupting the market and social order, while others praise them for enhancing China's market economy, pushing for the establishment of new institutions. Even though many of the current business owners have not received much education, as they can earn so much more money doing business than going to school, they are experts in their own fields, learning from experience and contacts with different types of people. Of course, the younger generation receives much better education as a result of the social and economic capital their parents have created for them.

The flexibility of the Wenzhou model also lies in the supportive policies of the local government. Wenzhou's private economy never really disappeared, despite different political movements and campaigns. This is partly because of the protection they enjoyed from local officials, which often means ignoring orders from the central government. Here, the clientelist ties kick in. Both local government and local people have benefited from the development of a private economy in a historically remote and resource-destitute area.

### Shangyuan Village: Supplementing the Private with the Public

*A Shareholding Land Cooperative*
Although all urban land is owned by the state, in rural China, a two-tier land tenure system has been adopted. Land is owned by the rural collective, but since the implementation of the household responsibility system, a bundle of property rights – such as the right to use, reap benefit from, and rent the land – have been transferred to individual households. However, in villages such as Huaxi and Nanjie, no property rights have been transferred to individuals in exchange for the provision of social welfare and public goods. In these cases, the rural collectives are able to plan the layout of the villages and allocate land for village-owned enterprises; economies of scale can be derived from pooling the precious land together. This is the path to industrialization in many of the villages with strong local governments.

In Wenzhou, with its business tradition, agriculture has never been the backbone of the economy. The development of household businesses does not require pooling the land. As a result, it is reasonable to expect that rural Wenzhou would be a strict follower of the household responsibility system.

However, several villages in Wenzhou retain control over the use of land, and Shangyuan Village is one of them. The land system in Shangyuan is close to a "shareholding land cooperative," or "land for shares" (*gutian zhi*) in which the village government collects contracted lots from villagers, consolidates them into larger tracts, and then rents them to third parties. Villagers' land rights are converted into shares in this land cooperative, and villagers are entitled to dividends derived from the income generated by the land. Shangyuan, by reconsolidating the land, built five commercial units – an electrical equipment market, a nonferrous metal market, a department store, a multipurpose building, and a parking lot – to collect rent. Ten percent of the revenue goes to insurance including villagers' medical insurance, 20 percent goes to property management, 30 percent is reserved in the collective fund, and the remaining 40 percent is distributed to the villagers as dividends. In addition, every villager is paid 1,480 yuan a year as a subsistence fee, since they are left with no farmland to produce crops.

This land system is different from Huaxi and Nanjie in that villagers' profits from their property rights are clearly defined, and the local government serves more like a broker than an executive board. There are no village-owned and operated enterprises, and people do not rely solely on the village for jobs and social welfare, although a successful collective economy – consisting mainly of rental markets – can provide them with a safety net.

### An Overview of the Village

Shangyuan, with a population of 1,475 (358 households),[7] covers an area of 0.56 square kilometers (roughly 138 acres). The net asset value of the village collective amounted to over 650 million yuan (more than US$78 million based on 2004 exchange rate) in 2004 with an annual growth rate of about 10 percent, and more than 11 million yuan was distributed to villagers as dividends.[8] The village has more than 200 household workshops, 80 shareholding cooperatives, 15 joint ventures, and 22 foreign-exchange earning enterprises (*chukou chuanghui qiye*), while over a third of the villagers work in the non-agricultural sector. Almost every household owns a business, and the average annual per capita income was over 31,800 yuan (roughly US$3,800) in 2005, excluding the incomes from private businesses (Figure 4.2).

Unlike Huaxi and Nanjie, land was contracted out to villagers in Shangyuan as early as 1979, with each person getting less than 0.3 mu of land, and the lease was for 15 years at the time. The released laborers

---

[7] Based on the village's survey in 2006.
[8] The village's brochure.

Figure 4.2. Apartment buildings in Shangyuan. Photo by the author.

started to build household workshops to produce electrical and hardware supplies. The village reallocated the land in 1983, assigning 60 mu
of land for widening the Route 104 highway (*guodao*) and building infrastructure. Four years later, villagers volunteered to contract their land to
an efficient grain-growing farmer in Dongfeng Village, and the farmer
in turn provided them with subsistence grains. In 1992, however, the
village government tried to convince each villager to turn in the land
they leased to have an electrical equipment market built in Shangyuan.
The village, in return, promised each resident an annual subsistence fee
of 400 yuan for each mu of land. The same year, Shangyuan Mansion of
Electrical Equipment was built with an annual revenue of 120,000 yuan.
By 1993, all the land was leased back to the village, thus completing the
collectivization of land use. Each villager in turn receives what is called
"collective living allowance" (*jiti shenghuo butie*)[9] as the collective part of
the economy grows.

Different from other parts of Wenzhou, villagers in Shangyuan relied
on agriculture during the Maoist era. Its high agricultural output made

[9]   The per capita annual allowance was 4,000 yuan as of 2007.

it a model party branch (*dang zhibu*)[10] in the planned economy.[11] There were no industries before the 1950s, and villagers made handicrafts or processed subsidiary food such as tofu, rice noodles, preserved eggs, and snacks to supplement agriculture. After the 1950s, there were several collectively organized businesses. In 1983, the party branch reallocated the land and opened streets to provide each household with retail space. Over 100 households started to make electrical and hardware products, such as outlets, switches, and sockets, at the back of the house and sold the products at the front (*qiandian houfang*). In 1986, a dozen household workshops began to improve the quality of their products and turned the workshops into modern businesses, hiring technicians and engineers from other places to help with their design and production. They developed into leading nationwide corporations such as Chint (Chinese name *Zhengtai*) and Delixi. In fact, the ten largest low-voltage electrical equipment companies, with an output value of over 100 million yuan, are all located in Shangyuan. They are the pride of the village and of all the private entrepreneurs. The village party secretary, Hu Chengyun, told me that Shangyuan's sales volume of these products accounts for about two-thirds of the national market.

The development of various markets and industries increased the house prices in Shangyuan. As a result, the retail space that each household was allocated can now bring in hundreds of thousands of yuan of rent per year – a fixed income for every household, thanks to the collective sector of the economy. Of course, the existence of many successful private enterprises provides jobs to local people and migrant workers and also drives the overall development of the village and neighboring places.

As Shangyuan is located in the town center, much of the change in its layout is closely related to the decisions of the Liushi township government. For example, in 1986 the town along with the Yueqing County Industrial Committee (*Yueqingxian Gongye Weiyuanhui*) decided to establish a demonstration electrical equipment factory,[12] and they picked its site in Shangyuan west of Liushi Bus Terminal near the Route 104 highway. After the negotiations between the township government and the village, Shangyuan allocated 6.5 mu of land for the construction of Liushi Electrical Equipment General

---

[10]  Any organizations with more than three but fewer than fifty Communist Party members, once approved by an upper-level party committee, can establish a party branch. Usually with more than 100 party members, a party committee can be formed.

[11]  Interview with Hu Zhixin, member of the party branch, in 2006.

[12]  A demonstration factory or enterprise is usually established as a showcase to guide other businesses in the industry; it was often used in China in the early years of the market reforms.

Factory. In 1986, the then party secretary Hu Zhifa was appointed to work at the Liushi Industrial Trading Company[13] and became Shangyuan's party secretary again in 1993 after the village party branch members signed and submitted an application to the town asking it to consider transferring Hu back. In 1990, Shangyuan allocated another 20 mu of land for the town to build its industrial district. Three years later, the town wanted to expropriate more land for the construction of infrastructures at a price of 27,000 yuan per mu. Because of Hu's experience as a town cadre and his previously established authority in the village, the leadership managed to persuade the villagers to agree with the acquisition and struck a deal with the town. Funding for building the various collectively owned marketplaces mainly came from the land acquisition fees paid by the town. Of course, in return, the town offered Shangyuan preferential policies such as approving the construction of the markets and making Shangyuan the demonstration site for building the new socialist countryside. Land acquisition often gives peasants a lump sum of money but, at the same time, deprives them of the source of sustainable future earnings – land. In Shangyuan, however, villagers pool together the land acquisition fees and the remaining land to develop a collective economy that continues to provide them with an income. As the Chinese proverb goes, "Give a man a fish and he will eat for a day. Teach him how to fish and he will eat for a lifetime." Only in the case of Shangyuan, fishing is not taught by others but rather a result of cadres' initiative and villagers' consensus that builds into a social contract in the village.

Therefore, each household in Shangyuan has at least three types of property: the old house built by the villagers themselves before land was leased back to the village, the retail space allocated by the village, and the apartment in the buildings constructed as part of the plan for creating a new socialist countryside. They call the apartment buildings "commercial residential buildings" (*shangpinfang*), and they were built in 1999 and 2002.

Ms. Zhang, director of the United Front Work Department of the Liushi Party Committee, told me that in the late 1980s and early 1990s many of the low-voltage electrical supplies were made by hand.

The products were shabby. Most of the family businesses would sell their products in front of the house and made them at the back. Since 1989 because the state strengthened quality control, family businesses were forced to adjust or close down.

---

[13] According to my interview with a town official, Ms. Zhang, the Industrial Trading Company was the previous Office for Industrial Development (*gongye bangongshi*) and is now called the TVE Administrative Office (*xiangzhen qiye guanli suo*). It is in charge of supervising the enterprises under the town's direct jurisdiction yet is not a part of the township government.

Besides, villagers could not earn much from farming, so they thought it was in their best interest (*you shihui*) to lease the land back to the village, since the village would provide them with houses and a subsistence fee (*kouliang kuan*).

Contrary to Huaxi and Nanjie, which are administrative villages comprised of a population with mixed surnames, Hu is the dominant family name in Shangyuan, accounting for about 80 percent of the population.[14] Therefore, it is a closely knit community where each person is related to others by blood, marriage, or education. The villagers, if not relatives, often went to the same school together. There is also an ancestral temple for the kin of Hu in the village with an annual revenue of over 600,000 yuan and voluntarily managed by the elderly. Scholarships are established for those in the Hu kinship network who have made it to college and gone on to graduate schools. The current party secretary, Hu Chengyun, who has been in the position since 2000, is also the legal representative of Delixi, as he is the younger cousin of the president of the company. During my stay in the village, Hu presented me with a newspaper listing all the important people with a Hu surname, which, of course, includes the current CCP general secretary, President Hu Jintao. They have a Hu-surname Association (*Hu Xing Xiehui*). Obviously, kinship networks still play a role in China and probably more so in Wenzhou.

In contrast with other parts of China, pursuing personal interests and seeking profits have had a long history in Wenzhou, and they seem to be well justified. The presence of various temples and churches throughout Wenzhou seems to confirm the Weberian thesis that the economy is intertwined with the cultural sphere. Many people in Wenzhou believe in religion, and Buddhism and Christianity are among the most popular types. This is not surprising, considering that Wenzhou was among the port cities opened to the West, including the activities of missionaries, after the Second Opium War[15] in 1876. The Christian population in Shangyuan, however, is very small, only two to three families; the majority of religious villagers believe in Buddhism and Taoism, most of whom are the elderly. There are two temples in the village for people to worship and burn incense. The only church, the Seventh-Day Adventist Church, was moved to the northwest of the Route 104 highway for the building of Shangyuan Electrical Equipment

---

[14] Interview with Hu Chengyun, the party secretary.

[15] The Second Opium War, or the Second Anglo-Chinese War, was a war led by the United Kingdom and France against the Qing Dynasty of China from 1856 to 1860 to expand their privileges in China and renegotiate the treaties signed after the First Opium War from 1839 to 1842.

Mansion in 1991. Many of my interviewees said that they have religious beliefs only because of their family legacy, and they do not actually study the Bible or the Buddhist classics. Especially for the younger members of the community, such religious beliefs are more inherited than adopted. Moreover, they are seen as mostly personal, and they do not appear to have any influence on the politics in the community.

Nevertheless, rituals at funerals and weddings, both of which are closely related to social and economic capital, are taken seriously by local people. Interviewees repeatedly told me that Wenzhou people are pragmatic; girls will only marry those who have three "zi's:" a house (*fangzi*, must be paid in full, not on a mortgage), a car (*chezi*), and savings (*piaozi*). When daughters of the successful private entrepreneurs get married, an extravagant dowry that often includes luxurious cars such as BMWs or Mercedes will be prepared, as wedding or funeral rituals are related to a family's "face" (*mianzi*). In this sense, Shangyuan villagers are both traditional and modern in that they use modern status symbols to practice traditional rituals that were once eradicated during the Maoist era.

Part of the reason collectivism is weak in Shangyuan is related to the fluidity of its labor force. In contrast to Huaxi or Nanjie villagers, who stay in their communities for jobs and welfare benefits, many of the villagers in Shangyuan constantly migrate to other places for business opportunities. They travel back and forth to sell and distribute their products, making an overarching set of values hard to establish and institutionalize. As a result, they form their own groups based on family and kinship ties or business alliances, which can provide them with more social and economic capital. That is also the reason there are many shareholding cooperatives in Shangyuan, as families pool their capital to expand their businesses. Such alliances are not formed under the visible hand of the government but rather out of voluntary association. Nonetheless, social organization in Shangyuan is not dissolved because of the collective part of the economy that provides the villagers with a safety net, public goods, and protection. Migrant workers are also better managed than many other villages in Wenzhou as a result of the existence of an effective government that keeps records of the floating population and supports a team of village security guards on a twenty-four-hour patrol duty.

### Small Party, Big People
In Shangyuan Village cadres are required to be in their offices five days a week, and they each receive a set income from the village budget. This includes a monthly salary of 700 yuan, a monthly allowance of 50 yuan

for no absences, 50 yuan gas allowance, 150 yuan medical fee, and 500 yuan telecommunication fee for the party secretary and village director and 300 yuan for other cadres. All the income and cadres' contact information are publicized in the brochure *Shangyuan Village Documents for Building Democracy and the Rule of Law (Shangyuancun minzhu fazhi jianshe ziliao)*.

Compared to the large bureaucracy in Huaxi and Nanjie, Shangyuan only has five Party Branch Committee members (*dangzhibu weiyuan*) and nine Villagers' Committee members (*cunmin weiyuanhui weiyuan*). In order to have more people involved in the decision-making process, the village stipulates that elected Party Branch Committee members cannot run for the election of Villagers' Committee. This is very different from Huaxi and Nanjie where leadership of the village, the Party, and the corporate often overlaps. The village only has forty-five party members, most of whom joined the Party at school or in the army, and very few party members have been recruited in the village.[16] Also, in contrast to Huaxi and Nanjie, almost every cadre in Shangyuan has a second job in addition to his or her office. Most of their income comes from their private businesses or board positions rather than their fixed salaries as cadres. For example, as mentioned earlier, Hu Chengyun, the party secretary, is the legal representative of Delixi, one of the top low-voltage electrical equipment producers in China.

The village also takes pride in its almost nonexistent reception expenses. All the visitors must arrange for their own board and lodging, or the village cadres may pay out of their own pocket, but never from the village's collective account. In Shangyuan, therefore, one does not see the omnipresent power of the village government as can be observed in Huaxi and Nanjie where it penetrates into every detail of people's lives. Despite having a collective sector, government in Shangyuan only plans the overall layout of the village, and each household lives on its own, and it does not run any of the businesses, but instead, contracts them out to collect rent and management fees. A perfect example that demonstrates these differences in power is my ability to retrieve my questionnaires. In Huaxi and Nanjie, I was able to get all 180 questionnaires back through the village bureaucracy, but in Shangyuan I was only able to manage a 40 percent return of the questionnaires through its bureaucratic system. Comparing the building of the government with that of the Delixi Group, a major private enterprise in the village, one can also get a sense of the relative wealth and power of the two (Figure 4.3, Figure 4.4).

---

[16] Interview with Hu Zhixin, party branch member in charge of party organization.

Figure 4.3. The building where Shangyuan Party Branch and Villagers' Committee are located. Photo by the author.

Figure 4.4. The headquarters of the Delixi Group in Shangyuan. Photo by the author.

Nevertheless, the village government, namely the Party Branch Committee and the Villagers' Committee, is in charge of the distribution of dividends and other social welfare benefits. Hu Chengyun told me that every major decision should first be discussed among members of the two committees, then be passed on to the party members, and finally get approved at the Villagers' Meeting (*cunmin dahui*). According to Hu, the major conflict was about who should get the welfare benefits. Some who have left the village or were married to urban residents also wanted to get a share of the collective money. The policies in Shangyuan are similar to Nanjie and Huaxi, which are virilocal. For example, if households have two daughters, only one can stay as a Shangyuan villager to enjoy the benefits; if the husband is registered as a rural resident, and the wife is registered as an urban resident, the wife can transfer her *hukou* to Shangyuan, but not the other way round. College graduates who choose to come back can enjoy the villager status; however, if they have passed the civil service exams (*gongwuyuan kaoshi*) and become a civil servant, their benefits will be revoked. The same is true for those who do not return within a year from their graduation. To encourage the execution of the family-planning policy, an only child in a family will be given double the amount of money. Like the cadres' income, how collective money is spent and distributed is publicized to the villagers. In Nanjie and Huaxi where villagers depend on the collective for jobs and salaries, governments have relatively larger bargaining power in comparison to the villagers and can thus exert coercive forces to require conformity. However, in Shangyuan, as villagers are not employed by the collective, they demand more transparency in terms of how money is spent and who qualifies for what benefits.

Hu Chengyun commented that the Huaxi model only has one peak, that is the collective, but in Shangyuan, there are countless peaks.

In Huaxi, nobody plunges into the commercial sea [*xiahai*, meaning running their own businesses]. Where there is pressure, there is motivation. Shangyuan people are more innovative and motivated. For us, it is better to be the head of a dog than a tail of the lion (*ningzuo jitou, buzuo fengwei*). Even if we have countless money to spend, we will still work on expanding our businesses.[17]

For Hu, however, without any preferential policies that collective enterprises such as Huaxi enjoy, Shangyuan still maintains a high standard of living. Does it mean that it is the perfect combination of private entrepreneurship and a collective safety net? Is the collective economy in Shangyuan more

---

[17] The justification of the pursuit of wealth through hard work in Wenzhou is similar to some aspects of the Protestant work ethic that Weber (1904–1905) describes.

viable and sustainable, given the current trends in China amid an increasingly globalized economy?

I think in analyzing the Wenzhou model, there are several things that we need to demystify. First, although the influence of the party ideology is weak in Wenzhou, it does not mean that local government as an institution is equally weak. In fact, the existence of a Wenzhou model is the result of local governments bargaining, hiding, and even deceiving the upper-level administrations to protect a private economy, and those red-hat collectives were exactly the invention of Wenzhou. Therefore, there is a strong clientelist tie between the administration and private entrepreneurs. In Shangyuan, Hu Chengyun made it clear on several occasions that the village government's major task was to serve Chint and Delixi so that they would not have to worry about anything other than the development of their businesses. The private enterprises, in turn, provide jobs and revenues to the locality, as well as political, and sometimes economic, capital to the cadres. Hu said that without Chint and Delixi there would be no Shangyuan, but obviously it can also be said the opposite; without the village assigning land for the two enterprises and the construction of the infrastructure, the enterprises would not be successful either.

Some people have started to pay attention to the increasing number of associations in Wenzhou – especially the Wenzhou Chambers of Commerce that have spread all over the world – wondering if these organizations will lead to a civil society that would replace some of the functions of the government. Based on my interviews, it seems that government still plays a much larger role than the Chambers of Commerce. Many of my respondents said that most of the Chambers of Commerce are only a name (*liuyu xingshi*) that do not have real functions. When asked if the Chamber can help bargain with the government, they answered that if their businesses perform well, the government will give them support, and they do not really need to go through an intermediary organization. According to them, the overseas Wenzhou Chambers of Commerce are similar to the associations for people from the same hometown (*tongxianghui*). The only cases in which the Chamber is helpful involve incidents such as the new regulations of the European Union (EU) on the production of cigarette lighters. Here, the expenses of the negotiations with the EU over the trade barriers need to be shared by all the enterprises involved, depending on the benefits they will gain from winning the litigation.

Second, Wenzhou's widespread private entrepreneurship has evolved over a long time and has its specific cultural and historical roots; therefore, it does not mean that a collectivist model is unattractive to the local

Table 4.2. *Attitudes toward a collective economy across villages*

How important do you think a collective economy is:
1) Very important 2) Important 3) Neutral 4) Not very important
5) No need at all

|  | Nanjie | Huaxi | Shangyuan |
|---|---|---|---|
| Mean | 1.76 | 1.41 | 1.58 |
| Standard deviation | 0.87 | 0.69 | 0.51 |

people, but that collectivism in the style of Nanjie and Huaxi will meet with greater resistance in Wenzhou. As a result, villages such as Shangyuan develop their own collectivism, and people in other parts of Wenzhou build their safety net through family and kinship ties. I was frequently told by my interviewees that being a government official – or as it is now called, a civil servant – is appealing because they consider the job "an iron rice bowl." When asked about how important they think a collective economy is in the questionnaire, all of the respondents in Shangyuan chose that it is important or very important; the percentage is higher than that of Nanjie but lower than Huaxi (Table 4.2), although the same respondents almost unanimously believed that the policy of "encouraging some people to get rich first" (*rang yibufenren xian fuqilai*) is a very good one (Table 4.3). It seems that despite the boldness and persistence that Wenzhou people have as entrepreneurs, many still prefer some kind of stability.

People in Wenzhou are probably the closest to the neoclassical assumption of *homo economicus*. They have very sharp business acumen and work to maximize their profits. As Hu Zhixin said, "in collective enterprises, each individual probably can only get 5 yuan out of every 100 yuan of profit; however, if I have my own business, all 100 yuan, deducting the taxes, will be mine. Who doesn't want to have their own businesses, if policy allows?" They can also be pretty self-interested. As Sun Yi, a second-generation private entrepreneur, said, "Wenzhou people may clean the floors of their houses three times a day, yet pour the dirty water on to the street." After several failed attempts to interview the villagers, one of my local contacts tried to comfort me, saying that "people [in Wenzhou] can be a little aloof (*renqing youdian lengmo*); people think differently (*sixiang buyiyang*)." "Where there is a profit, there are Wenzhou people" actually implies that "where there are no profits, people will be scarce."

Table 4.3. *Attitudes toward the policy of "encouraging some people to get rich first" across villages*

What do you think of the policy of "encouraging some people to get rich first"?
1) Very bad 2) Not good 3) Have both advantages and disadvantages
4) Good 5) Very good

|  | Nanjie | Huaxi | Shangyuan |
|---|---|---|---|
| Mean | 3.17 | 4.18 | 4.90 |
| Standard deviation | 0.92 | 0.82 | 0.30 |

Nevertheless, they are still social beings, not just *homo economicus*. The way they organize their economy is perhaps the closest to the traditional Chinese peasant economy (*xiaonong jingji*) based on what Fei Xiaotong calls "concentric differentiation."[18] Very few foreign-invested firms or nonlocal firms can penetrate into Wenzhou's market, because of the "unfavorable investment environment," otherwise known as intense local competition.

Therefore, Wenzhou's exclusivism, on the other hand, demonstrates their bond. Entrepreneurs help each other to survive in the market. There are many cases of relatives or friends pooling their resources to open a business, and after they have all gained experience and accumulated capital, they will separate and run their own businesses to expand the industry and enhance the competitiveness of Wenzhou products as a whole. For example, the presidents of Chint and Delixi were schoolmates, and they used to run a switchgear factory together from 1984 to 1991. Then the factory was divided into two companies. The president of the well-known shoe company, Hongqingting (Red Dragonfly), once worked for his friend and nephew-in-law, the president of the biggest shoe company in China, Aokang, and then pulled out his capital and opened his own business. Through imitating and learning from others and healthy competition, the private economy expands. Moreover, without any access to state-controlled bank loans and other sources of financing, entrepreneurs in Wenzhou have developed their own ways to raise funds: from individual loans, self-organized credit

---

[18] Fei (1986), a famous Chinese anthropologist and sociologist, describes Chinese society as the ripples created when a stone is thrown into the lake, and the concentric rings flowing out from the center are social relationships. Everyone stands in the center of the circles created by their social influence. The rings near the center are kinship relationships, and the closer to the center, the more important the relationship. People's treatment of others will depend on the closeness of the relationship.

unions and private banks at the early stage to today's shareholding cooperatives. This lending and borrowing is based on not only contracts and interest rates but also trust and reputation.

The Wenzhou model, however, encounters several challenges. First, like
Huaxi and Nanjie, each household firm is faced with the "intrusion" of outsiders as business grows and market competition becomes more intense.
When nepotism is not efficient any more, new ties and institutions must be
formed.

Second, as Wenzhou has a strong culture of grassroots entrepreneurship, people have little motivation to get formal education. Their education
level is incommensurate with their wealth and so are the infrastructure,
health facilities, and other public goods. The success of the first generation
of Wenzhou entrepreneurs is a result of their earlier start than the rest of
China – the timing, their endurance during hardships, and their ability to
seize market opportunities as they moved around the country when population mobility in China was still highly restricted and limited. However,
as other places start to catch up and information flows more easily, they
may be losing their comparative advantage, especially when some of the
younger generations, growing in a much wealthier environment, are not as
hardworking as their parents.

Third, some people doubt that this model can contribute to China's overall development, as Wenzhou businesspeople seem to be grabbing wealth
from other parts of China, while the rest of the country is sharing their
risks. Successful private enterprises like Chint and Delixi can, of course,
provide jobs and even take on certain social responsibilities, but thousands
of other emigrants are still vendors and peddlers, not that different from
other migrant workers. In addition, small private businesses are often still
involved in labor-intensive, low value-added industries with a small profit
margin and have to rely on cutting cost to squeeze profit. Such businesses
are often export oriented and serve as the subcontractors of large multina-
tional corporations subject to foreign demand and price competition from
other parts of China and the world. The building of public goods and the
regulation of economic activities need a strong community, and the power
of organization cannot be underestimated. In this sense, Shangyuan Village
has probably started to make a first step in this direction.

# FIVE

# Back to the Future

## Community Capitalism and the Search
## for Alternatives

In our days, everything seems pregnant with its contrary: Machinery, gifted with the wonderful power of shortening and fructifying human labour, we behold starving and overworking it; The newfangled sources of wealth, by some strange weird spell, are turned into sources of want; The victories of art seem bought by the loss of character. At the same pace that mankind masters nature, man seems to become enslaved to other men or to his own infamy. Even the pure light of science seems unable to shine but on the dark background of ignorance. All our invention and progress seem to result in endowing material forces with intellectual life, and in stultifying human life into a material force.

Marx (Speech, April 14, 1856)

Throughout the history of the Chinese Communist Party, it seems to have been a firm believer in manpower and its ability to transform and defeat nature. In the reform era, the fight has been extended to include not just the battle against nature but also the struggle against the market. China is learning not only to dance with the market, but also to tame it. Although the country has successfully become the workshop of the world as a result of its vast and cheap labor supply and transformed itself into a major player in the global market, the CCP cannot yet declare victory over either nature or the market. Underlying its economic achievements, critics are quick to point out China's potential problems: economic bubbles, slow political reform, increasing social inequality, and environmental degradation, to name just a few. While the great economic achievements over a short period of time have brought many Chinese hope and confidence, and others doubt or even fear, institutional innovations at the grassroots indicate the wisdom of the masses and the adaptability of local communities. Where should China be heading? What can it tell us about the market and society? What lessons can we draw from the local experiences? To answer these questions, let us first go back to the three different, yet comparable, strategies of rural development

121

described in the previous chapters – those derived from Nanjie, Huaxi, and Shangyuan – by looking at their ownership structures, institutional setups, and sense-making mechanisms.

## Ownership Structures

China's land ownership is fundamentally public. In the cities, land is owned by the state, whereas in the villages, land is officially owned by the collective, a policy leftover from the commune era. However, ownership includes a bundle of separate rights such as the right of control, the right to income, and the right of transfer (Walder 2011), which gives rise to hybrid forms of ownership that transcend the dichotomy between private and public. In China a bundle of property rights has been transferred to peasants in most of the villages by means of leasing. They can use the land, decide what to grow on the land, and reap its harvest. Compensation is received if their land needs to be expropriated for some other purposes, but they cannot individually sell or buy land or borrow against it as a mortgage for cash to invest in tools, machinery, or other products. Although private property rights are now protected by law, the state's policy toward rural land is unlikely to change in the near future. The collective ownership of rural land is partly to prevent it from getting concentrated into a few hands and to provide peasants with the means of basic subsistence so that even though they leave for the cities they still have the land to hold on to. Nonetheless, there have been an increasing number of land disputes in recent years, mostly because peasants are often undercompensated, if at all compensated, when their land is expropriated by the local government or private real estate developers backed by local officials. The central and local states have essentially become the largest landlords that profit from selling or leasing land for commercial uses, which often involves corruption and collusion, while peasants have not received a fair share of the yields. Although land disputes are not within the scope of this book, how land is utilized has a tremendous impact on the lives of the peasants.

While land is collectively owned, the use of land in many villages has been privatized, although the village can adjust land distribution at the end of each lease. However, the use of land is also collectively owned in the cases of Nanjie and Huaxi, whereas in Shangyuan the use right is leased back to the collective so that the village can be planned as a whole. Each household in Shangyuan in turn gets a storefront that it can either rent to others or use to run its own businesses, an apartment, and dividends from the collectively owned rental markets.

Table 5.1. *Economic flow and ownership structure*

|  | Nanjie | Huaxi | Shangyuan |
|---|---|---|---|
| Production | Collective | Collective | Collective + Private |
| Distribution | Market | Market | Market |
|  | Redistribution (quasi-egalitarian) | Redistribution (differential) | Redistribution (rent distribution) |
| Consumption | Fixed proportion of profits (little cash) | Fixed proportion of income, bonus and dividends | Personal decision (minus the village's maintenance costs) |

If we analyze the three villages by their patterns of economic flow – production, distribution, and consumption – the structure of different property rights leads to different paths (Table 5.1). For Nanjie and Huaxi, the factors of production (land, labor, capital, technology, and organization) are controlled by the village as a large collectively owned corporation. For Shangyuan, only land and a certain amount of capital and organization are controlled by the collective, as private household businesses are prevalent, and land is pooled together as the villagers' investment, which generates dividends according to their share of the land.

Distribution in Nanjie and Huaxi, however, is twofold: as corporations, products are distributed through exchanges on the market, although personal networks (*guanxi*) often exert influence on market transactions; as a community, resource allocation adopts a redistributive mechanism by means of the social welfare system. Shangyuan is similar, except for the fact that the market plays a larger role and redistribution is limited to dividends and houses as a result of pooling land together.

For consumption, what portion of the profits should be put into production and what portion into consumption is determined by the collective in Nanjie and Huaxi, or more specifically, by the leadership; therefore, saving and reinvestment in production is mandatory, although in Nanjie the villagers' purchasing power is further restricted because of the low disposable income. Nevertheless, the community provides its members with the necessities of life and basic consumer products such as food, furnished apartments, Internet access, and so on; in Huaxi, such products even extend to automobiles. Therefore, people do not need to spend much cash while staying in the village. Shangyuan, however, does not have village-run enterprises, so whether to consume or reinvest is more of a personal decision. Of course, different village cultures and geographic locations also influence people's consumption behaviors. In Nanjie, for example, people's lives are generally simple, and that is why when Gu Yi's parents bought what was regarded by the villagers as a large amount of meat, they were thought to be purchasing for the village's canteen not for their own consumption. Similarly in Huaxi, although villagers live in luxurious villas furnished with all kinds of modern conveniences, most are still very thrifty. When I visited their homes, I saw the leftovers from previous meals kept under mesh food covers including some dried fish and pickles. Like most Chinese, they hung their clothes on clotheslines to dry instead of using dryers. Generational differences also exist. In Shangyuan, for instance, parents are willing to pay for their children's extravagant weddings and dowries, while they themselves tend to save rather than spend.

As a result, we cannot simply divide property rights into collective and private categories, for all agricultural land is collectively owned, but the way of organizing property rights varies. Property rights alone cannot really determine the effectiveness of an economy, as all three villages, despite different ownership structures, provide their villagers with relatively comfortable living conditions, and the process of adjusting property rights is a function of traditions, state policies, local cultures, and the power of different interest groups.

## Institutional Structures

North (1981) points out the importance of the state in facilitating institutional change through defining property rights and effecting institutionalized norms to reduce transaction costs. Nee (2005) calls the current path of development in China, politicized capitalism, or state capitalism, as the state's control over resources lingers on. From the three cases, we can see that changes in state policies lead to changes in the organization of local communities, no matter whether it is in Maoist China or in the reform era.

However, unlike old institutionalism, new institutionalism emphasizes not only the "top-down" process described by scholars like North but also the "bottom-up" character of institutional formation (Scott 2001: 196). In other words, although institutions are often diffused from the top and internalized by individuals at the grassroots, local people also have their own room for creativity, as they can choose what institutions to pay attention to and what to ignore, convert them to fit into local conditions, or interpret them in their own ways. Therefore, it is also important to take into account the local state, as the same state policies often give rise to distinct ways of social and economic organization. Local communities are in a constant bargaining process with the state for attention and resources and to maintain their identities.

In transitional China, during the dual transformation – from an agrarian society to an industrial society and from a planned economy to a market economy – there have been various paths of development. Both Nanjie and Huaxi, which have thriving collective economies and receive abundant state resources, have strong local governments, especially party apparatuses. They participate in market exchanges, but still maintain a relatively closely knit community because of the villagers' dependence on the collective and the boundary set between villagers and non-villagers that has evolved into a unique group identity. The local government, led by the village party secretary, exerts power very similar to that of a patriarch, and the entire village is managed as if it were an extended family, although the inhabitants may not necessarily have any blood relationships. Villagers rely on the government, or the patriarch, for living and jurisdiction, and the government represents the villagers to compete for state resources and make "rational" economic decisions. Unlike in prototypical capitalism, government both sets rules and controls resources for production, and it is equally a political and an economic actor.

However, the relative importance of market and redistribution varies between Nanjie and Huaxi, and their internal management is distinct. The leadership in Nanjie believes that monetary rewards can trigger the endless pursuit of self-interest and are thus detrimental to the collective. As a result, the incentive structure is based more on ideal and moral interests than on material interests, although the government seems to realize the limits of moral appeals, and thus the ten-star model family contest and the Village Code of Conduct both resort to economic sanctions. Nevertheless, the village cadres emphasized that such economic sanctions were nominal; the real pressure came from losing face in a closely knit community. The incentives for villagers to obey the rules and support the norms and values of the organization include the ideal incentive that the village will be built into "a communist heaven," which appeals to those who are nostalgic for the "good old days" in Maoist China and also informs the villagers that they are working for a righteous cause with a noble end; the moral incentive that the whole village is a common interest group so that the failure of one leads to that of others, with the same argument applying to success (*yi rong ju rong, yi sun ju sun*); the material incentive of getting a high standard of living; and the status incentive of being promoted to important positions or respected by fellow villagers. Similarly, Cui Zhiyuan ([1998] 2000), taking a game theory perspective, argues that the reasons Nanjie can overcome the free rider problem are because it has leaders that set good examples and make a real commitment to the collectivist economy, the cooperation-inducing expectations in repeated games that make "one for all and all for one" more appealing than free riding, and the team incentive scheme that bind members' gains and losses in non-repeated games such as those involving migrant workers.

One of the problems with the incentive structure in Nanjie is that after the economy has reached a certain level, there might be little motivation for the villagers to continue the same pace of development. This is because the distribution system is not correlated with profits – that is, more profits do not result in more income or much higher social welfare – because the income is almost fixed, and the welfare system has already covered most of people's necessities. Also, the same incentive structure for all is deemed ineffective, and at the end of the day, only those satisfied with the status quo, and oftentimes the weaker members – those who are least productive, competitive, and ambitious – will stay, which is harmful for keeping up the momentum for innovation. For cooperatives such as Israeli kibbutzim, the commonwealth system is maintained through common values and beliefs while members are more equal and organization is flatter. In Nanjie, however, common values are upheld as a result of the respected patriarchal leader and the boundary created to form a common interest group. Therefore, I would argue that the continuity of the Nanjie model lies in how much villagers internalize the collectivist values so that even without the patriarchal leader they will not deviate from the current path.

Huaxi, however, has a more complex system of rewards, so the material incentive is stronger, as villagers are both workers and shareholders. They have constantly invested their labor and capital in the collective economy because of the forced reinvestment and the fact that most of their money cannot be converted into cash. As a result, the longer one stays in the village, the less likely one will leave, as the price of departure is much higher than in Nanjie. Meanwhile, the expansion of the original village to include its neighboring villages provides greater social cohesion, especially among the original villagers, giving them more moral and status incentives. The problem with Huaxi lies in its social integration: how to combine people getting different rewards and have them contribute with equal passion to the system, as there is no ideal incentive.

Both Huaxi and Nanjie, in a way, are not that different from many large family businesses in Japan and South Korea that have a smart and highly respected leader, a management style similar to the military, and an

Table 5.2. *Different models of social and economic integration*

|  | Nanjie | Huaxi | Shangyuan |
|---|---|---|---|
| Role of the local state | Centralized; set rules and control resources for production | Centralized; set rules and control resources for production | Decentralized; set rules and control only land |
| Incentive structure | More moral and ideal than material | Material and moral | Mainly material with moral obligations to family and kin |
| Analogy | The military | A conglomerate (e.g., Japanese *keiretsu*) | An ethnic enclave |

emphasis on collective goals over individual interests. Whether Nanjie will become like Huaxi depends on how much it can hold on to its communist ideology and the quasi-egalitarian distribution system that has little to do with one's abilities and achievements.

Shangyuan does not have as strong local government, partly because of its location in Wenzhou, which the state designated as the experimental zone for a private economy. Meanwhile, as a result of Wenzhou's model of the "cluster economy," Shangyuan is able to take advantage of the industry for electrical equipment and profits from building marketplaces to collect rent. In this way, the government has very little control over the resources needed for production except in the case of land and mainly serves to set rules, which is close to the role of government in typical capitalist systems. The management of economic and social activities is more diffuse than that in Nanjie and Huaxi, and each household controls itself in terms of production and daily lives. However, such a way of organization is not completely individualistic, as kinship ties replace the patriarchal government. The major incentive is material rather than moral; yet, the moral responsibilities to family and kin also come into play (Table 5.2). Moreover, the expanding collective sector in its economy requires stronger community leadership and will probably revitalize people's community identity; therefore, rather than being an individual with a family network or being a Wenzhou person, people will probably increasingly regard their identity as a Shangyuan villager as their master status.

## Culture and Social Networks

Social transformations are often restricted by past and existing institutional structures, described in the literature as "structural inertia" or "path dependency." Culture and values are part of the normative structures that can influence the direction of development. Swedberg, borrowing from Weber, gives a clear description of the cultural aspect of economic action:

*valuation* and *sense-making* ... (1) anything economic is typically viewed as being either positive or negative, and (2) economic phenomena, like all human phenomena, have somehow to be pieced together in the human mind in order to make sense and acquire a distinct *Gestalt.* (2005: 25)

As market forces are introduced, the previously held socialist values are greatly challenged. Therefore, people need new sense-making mechanisms to evaluate the reality: Why should we make money? How should we make money? What happens after we have made money?

In the cases of Nanjie and Huaxi, collectively owned enterprises legitimize profits, as they serve the public good, and borrowing the same institutional arrangement from recent times, the sense-making turns "immediate interest into 'interest properly understood'" (Swedberg 2005: 26). On the other hand, although a dualistic economic ethic is supposed to be detrimental to capitalist development, as members are honest only to fellow members, it is used in Shangyuan, and Wenzhou more generally, to cement community members together to compete with outsiders and as mutual assistance in the form of economies of scale, since a collective economy has never been strong. This culture was particularly useful in the early stage of capitalist development in Wenzhou.

Not only do institutional mechanisms constrain organizational practice and structure, individuals and organizations also innovate and contribute to institutional change. Informal social networks play an important role in the choices of paths to development. Here, it is necessary to analyze both the principal/agent networks and the agent/member networks, that is, the networks between the state and other upper-level government officials and local cadres, and the networks between local cadres and villagers. The former determines what kind of resources the local communities can mobilize, and the latter affects the incentive structure and the resource distribution mechanism employed in local communities.

In Nanjie and Huaxi, because of the party secretary's connections with upper-level governments, the villages have more political capital and social capital, which can bring to them information, business opportunities, tax deductions, or in the Nanjie case, direct access to bank loans. In Shangyuan, as a result of Wenzhou's overall lack of state support, villagers have to resort to their own resources. However, the location of Shangyuan in the town center and its previous party secretary's connection with the township government make the development of infrastructure such as highways and various marketplaces possible.

Within the communities, how close the villagers are and how strong the leadership is decides what kind of incentives the villages use to stabilize the social order and the ways of organizing economic and social resources. In all the three cases we can discover a distribution system dependent on group boundaries. Although it is only in the Shangyuan case that production is actually organized around family and kinship ties in the form of household firms, the stratification mechanisms used in Huaxi and Nanjie follow a similar pattern. People who have family or pseudo-family ties with the patriarch are promoted to the core of the leadership; more prestigious jobs are saved for villagers, and at the bottom of the social stratification system are the migrant workers. Furthermore, social welfare benefits are also distributed according to a person's closeness to the center of the village networks.

## The Rationality of Collectivism and Community Capitalism

As the world is struggling to escape from its deepest recession in decades with record high unemployment rates, stagnant economic growth, plunging consumer spending, and rising social tensions, there is an increasing debate over whether this showcases the curse of laissez-faire and the end of American-style capitalism. The new mantra "socialism for the rich, capitalism for the poor," although in many ways over-generalized and simplistic, does catch the core of this critique: surging social inequalities within and between nations and the blind worship of the magic of the "invisible hand." As governments in advanced capitalist countries in America and Europe start to talk about state intervention, regulations, and public-funded projects to stimulate the market and restore the socioeconomic order, it seems to be a perfect moment to consider alternative models of development and particularly the relationship between the state and the market. After all, capitalism is a way of organizing resources, and it is hardly surprising that there is not just one form of this economic arrangement as indicated in the vast amount of literature on varieties of capitalism that compares and contrasts American capitalism with capitalism in Germany, Japan, Scandinavian countries, and so on. Although modernization and globalization are often thought as forces that drive out alternative versions of capitalism, variants across time and space abound as capitalism is structured by economies, cultures, and polities, and further constrained by historical institutions (Streeck 2011). *Community capitalism* revealed in the three cases offers a new possibility in the "double movement" (Polanyi [1944] 1957) between the embedding and disembedding of the economic in the social, or between commodification and its backlash.

Weber suggests that in addition to the formal rationality of economic action, there is also the substantive rationality. It is

not sufficient to consider only the purely formal fact that calculations are being made on grounds of expediency by the methods which are, among those available, technically the most nearly adequate. In addition, it is necessary to take account of the fact that economic activity is oriented to ultimate ends (*Forderungen*) of some kind, whether they be ethical, political, utilitarian, hedonistic, the attainment of social distinction, of social equality, or of anything else. (1947: 185)

In all three cases, collectivism is *reasonable* and has its rationality, although it is not necessarily the most efficient way of production.

As I discussed in the chapter on Nanjie, collectivism solves the problem where both the state and the market fail. It prepares villagers for the transition from an agrarian society to an industrial society and pools resources to compete in the market that disadvantages the peasants. Instead of releasing the villagers to wander around in the cities looking for low-wage jobs and creating urban slums, collectivism keeps them both within the community and employed, and it helps transform the village as a whole. As one of my interviewees in Nanjie commented, "it is absurd to call the household responsibility system a great invention, because that was the way peasants had organized their production for thousands of years." For him, it is the collective economy in rural China that marks a breakthrough.

Of course, we can also see the influence of the transition of the larger social context on local communities. For example, in Nanjie and Huaxi, the traditional division between village elite and villagers was changed into a division of party leaders and villagers as the communist state penetrated the communities. When the market forces entered into the villages, a managerial elite started to form, and traditional farming was replaced by industrial production. In locations where the party apparatus is strong, the managerial elite will be recruited into the Party and join the political elite. Therefore, Huaxi and Nanjie emphasize that their leaders should be "capable" both politically and economically – that is, have both political and human capital. Human capital does not necessarily correlate with one's educational credentials but more to the individual's performance in managing the collective enterprises. As a result, either political leaders are converted into executives or executives are assimilated into the Party. For places like Shangyuan, where the party leadership is not strong, the economy and the maintenance of community social welfare are increasingly separated. In some villages social welfare has completely disappeared, and peasants care for their own. Shangyuan still keeps its community organization, mainly around the village elite who are elected into the party leadership. They secure a safety net for the private entrepreneurs who fight for survival in the market.

I argue that the alternative model that the three cases suggest is *community capitalism*, with the community serving as both a redistributive unit and an entity competing in the market. The system is sustained by group boundaries set between community members and outsiders, while collectivist values are used to justify and make sense of profit-making activities and the legitimacy of the model. Within the community, different governance structures can be applied ranging from more centralized organization such as that in Huaxi and Nanjie that emphasizes the leaders' accountability to their members in achieving common prosperity to more family-based one such as that in Shangyuan. Community capitalism transcends the dichotomy of the state and the market, autocracy and democracy, capitalism and communism. The household responsibility system that partially privatizes land rights can give peasants an incentive to increase agricultural productivity. However, the increase in productivity does not necessarily bring about economic development, more doubtfully, social development, especially where land is scarce and the population is dense and when subsistence farming is no longer viable. Collectivization of land rights is more conducive to community building and offers peasants the social welfare benefits that the market is eroding and the state is not yet capable of providing. Whether or not there should be collective enterprises depends on local tradition and leadership; however, it is necessary to have some kind of social organization that can provide public goods, and in a developing country as large and diverse as China, such a function can well be delegated to local communities. To some extent, the latest campaign of building a new socialist countryside is a call for the revival of community organization in rural China.

Although community capitalism may sound like an oxymoron, there are multiple factors that prevent the three villages from falling into the "tragedy of the commons," described by Hardin (1968), and from the situation where community is dissolved by capital. Although the initial collectivization was a result of historical contingencies such as the village leader's preference and the village's specific social and economic conditions, collectivism has been sustained as villagers form a common interest group. Internally, community members are taken care of and become stakeholders of the collective economy; externally, collectivism has become the community's goodwill or reputation and trustworthiness that can be converted into advantages in the market. Moreover, community serves as a base for bargaining for economic and political resources. Collectivism is further reinforced through common experiences in the village's uneven path toward development and in contrast with both its own historical past and outsiders. Therefore, a sense of in-group solidarity is developed in the process of boundary setting. Finally, collectivism becomes institutionalized through a social hierarchy that rewards conformity to a collective economy, an incentive system that combines collective and individual interests and makes disengagement costly, and an ideology that justifies profit making but at the same time emphasizes responsibilities to fellow members. Therefore, community capitalism is not built upon impartial love or universalism, and it does not mean that it cannot serve instrumental ends such as economic benefits. In fact, economic benefits may be one major source of its legitimacy. However, economic efficiency is often the by-product and certainly not the only goal or source of mobilization.

The three villages described in this book are industrial villages, but I think community capitalism can also be applied to villages where farming is still the dominant source of income, as investment in farming tools, seeds, and agricultural technologies is often beyond the financial abilities of individual families. In addition, the price fluctuations of agricultural produce in the global market and the lack of distribution channels often make small farmers vulnerable. We, thus, see the marginalization of small farmers worldwide. Community capitalism is probably a better solution than building the Chinese version of agribusiness, as corporatization deprives local farmers of their knowledge and decision making and their ability to keep the profits that they generate. Furthermore, it is not as rigid as the old commune system, as communities actively participate in the market and produce for profits, and members' interests are also taken into account.

Whether community capitalism can be a viable path for urban cities, especially megacities like Beijing and Shanghai, remains to be seen, as common values and interests are much more difficult to form and maintain in a more heterogeneous society with diverse interests. However, within the cities there are honeycomb communities, like ethnic enclaves in the United States and migrant enclaves and urban village enclaves (*chengzhongcun*) in China, where – to borrow Portes and Sensenbrenner's (1993) terms – bounded solidarity and enforceable trust are formed. Because of common experiences of adversities and/or shared identities, members of those enclaves support each other based on particularistic obligations and a similar cultural repertoire and thereby reinforce each other's social capital. This common sense of belonging propels members to go beyond self-interest in the market and sometimes engage in altruistic conduct within the enclave. The social capital developed, in turn, helps members financially and strengthens the community's economic competitiveness as a whole. This may be one possibility of how community capitalism can be practiced in an urban setting. Of course, how sustainable these urban communities are, and whether they will only stay as weapons of the weak, also depends on the state's urban policies and various institutions regarding development, land, residency, employment, and association.

Let me conclude with a few general lessons that we can draw from transitional China.

First, historical legacies and cultural traditions should not be dismissed. Many measures in the process of China's reform adopt preexisting institutions so that such reforms can be easily legitimized without any earth-shaking changes in the society. They provide people with sense-making mechanisms that maintain group identities during unprecedented social transformation.

Second, it is important to bring new incentives not only for private enterprises and individuals, but also for government agencies and officials. However, people oftentimes pay more attention to the former yet neglect the latter. In the three cases that I discuss in this book, especially the examples of Nanjie and Huaxi, cadres have invested themselves in the villages, and such commitment ensures the continuity of policies and avoids overlooking long-term development for short-term gains or rent-seeking activities on the cadres' part. Therefore, sometimes it is not about abolishing or opposing state involvement, but about adapting and incorporating it. Privatization is not the panacea for all problems and, in fact, may create difficulties for the weakest and most powerless groups in society. Therefore, social organization should be maintained to provide public goods.

Third, theories matter, but real practices often outwit rigid theories. The most important thing is to introduce the competition mechanism and provide a flexible environment for local innovation and variations. The three successful stories in these communities, although imperfect, reveal the folk wisdom in competing for and mobilizing resources, sometimes even through illegal or noninstitutionalized means. Changes in the formal institutions are often the result of informal practices and experiments. In this sense, the Chinese government is on the right track to allow local differences. As the state moves to further liberalize its economy and increasingly retreats from the social contract with its citizens, it may be time to deal with the "social deficits" (Pei 2009: 13) accumulated as a result of unrelenting economic growth. The collectivist villages in China could offer a new vision as the state rethinks its priorities of development.

With only three cases, it is hard to generalize the research findings to the whole nation, as there are enormous variations across geographic regions possessing different traditions, cultures, and natural conditions. However, each of the three cases indicates that the market and the state are not two opposite extremes; in fact, local communities create different combinations of the two to construct a path suitable to their own circumstances. Perhaps someday these star villages will fade into oblivion, but their experience, both successes and failures, will always provide valuable lessons.

# Methodology

Since I am more interested in the interaction between economic, social, and political institutions, my strategy in this research is similar to what Thomas B. Gold calls "a comprehensive approach":

> It can incorporate and link the findings of economists, historians, anthropologists, political scientists, and sociologists, locate them in a global context,[1] and answer critical questions that narrower approaches ignore. One does not plug data into preassembled boxes, but uses them as a guide to ask certain types of questions. (1986. 17)

I use both the grounded theory method and the interpretive case method. Grounded theory method offers observations and descriptions of a specific group of people and makes generalizations about their behavior over time and across different settings, in hope of developing better hypotheses or new taxonomies. However, this method is still fundamentally ahistorical, having no interest in generalizations about larger contexts. Therefore, I also apply the interpretive case method, which makes the same kind of observations as the grounded theory does, yet connects small observations to larger social and cultural themes.

The weakness of the two methods lies in their hermeneutic nature, meaning how the researcher portrays the situation and how he/she interprets it may be influenced by his/her own biases and interests. Therefore, different observers may have different interpretations of what is going on. To help balance my potentially biased observation, I tried to diversify the types of data to constantly check and refine my hypotheses, interview questions, and concepts.

---

[1] In my case, it would be more of a national context than a global context, but the goal is the same – to combine micro and macro analyses of both local and broader institutions.

The data in this book are largely based on my field research in the three villages in China. I visited Nanjie on five occasions. My first visit took place at the end of 2003, and I spent a week there. That was the first time I became intrigued by the village. I returned to the village in the summer of 2004 and was able to establish some contacts there. My third visit was in the winter of 2005, when I created a preliminary survey for some of the villagers to take, and also interviewed extensively. I went for the fourth time in the summer of 2006 with refined surveys and conducted in-depth interviews with thirty people, most of which were more than one hour in length. My interviewees include village cadres, county cadres, ordinary villagers, people from the neighboring area, and migrant workers. I also observed how people work, and attended several village-wide meetings. In the summer of 2010, I returned to the village to get updated information. I especially wanted to find out villagers' responses to the negative media coverage in 2008, if Nanjie had indeed changed its property ownership, and how it fared after the global recession.

Nanjie Village has a fairly complete and organized archiving system, so some of my data also come from the village archives, including village newspapers, records of the documents issued by the government, and voting results. Statistics of the employees, such as the demographic data and their salaries, however, are scattered throughout different offices. Sometimes even the village cadres did not know where to get the specific statistics I wanted. Therefore, I had to gather information from different sources and cross-check in order to create a clear picture of what was going on.

I spent six months in China in the year of 2006, conducting field research. Beside the time spent in Nanjie, I also visited Huaxi, Shangyuan, and other regions in or near Wenzhou. In 2010, I paid another visit to Huaxi, visiting some old contacts and doing further interviews with villagers and migrant workers.

Although my personal networks in those villages provided initial contacts and interviewees, especially with the help from local organizations like workers unions and youth leagues, further interviews depended on snowballing and random selection to get more diversified subjects and more objective answers. Observation of the villagers' everyday life and important meetings and events as well as the internal publications and archives were also a major source of information.

Originally I planned to interview thirty villagers in both Shangyuan and Huaxi. My plan was not able to be fulfilled in Shangyuan. There were two barriers. First, Shangyuan Village is not as hierarchical as the other two villages. People are mostly self-employed, and many of them were out doing business. Those who stayed in the village were mostly the elderly and migrant workers. In one of the stores, three teenagers were sitting there, answering telephones, while the parents were on a business trip out of the village. There was not a single place where you could find villagers gathering; people were floating about all the time. They were either too busy or simply not willing to accept any interviews. Second, the Wenzhou dialect is extremely hard to understand, and the elderly cannot really speak much Mandarin, so I had to conduct my interviews with two local contacts. With two interpreters present, it became even harder to get people to talk. Therefore, my interviewees in Shangyuan were mostly local officials and their friends. However, I was able to balance the view by interviewing ordinary people and entrepreneurs in the city of Wenzhou. Given the fact that people often talk about the whole region together as a "Wenzhou model," life in the city of Wenzhou can be a reference to life in Shangyuan. In addition, Wenzhou's economic achievements started from its thriving rural industries, so there are a lot of connections between urban and rural residents.

I also conducted surveys in the field, which helped me locate subjects for interviews, refine my interview questions, and get an overall picture of the villages. These surveys gather data on demographic variables in the villages and explore attitudes toward types of ownership, income distribution, government, economic and social policies, the relationship between officials and villagers, and plans for the future in different groups. The surveys were randomly sent to the villagers by villagers' teams (*cunmin xiaozu*),[2] and each village was distributed with 180 surveys. Except for Shangyuan, all the surveys in the other two villages were fully returned, although a small number of the surveys (less than 4 percent) were invalid with incomplete answers. Although the questionnaires are anonymous, I left a space for people to leave their contact information and also provided mine, should they be willing to be further interviewed. Some of the interviewees were recruited in this way.

---

[2] Under the Villagers' Committee, villagers are divided into several villagers' teams. Sometimes people who live in the same apartment building form a villagers' team, and each team has a head.

# APPENDIX B

# Map of Site Locations

# Bibliography

Amendment to the Constitution of the People's Republic of China. 1999, Article 16. Retrieved September 10, 2012 (http://www.china.org.cn/china/ LegislationsForm2001-2010/2011-02/12/content_21907042.htm).

Arrighi, Giovanni. 2007. *Adam Smith in Beijing: Lineages of the Twenty-First Century*. New York: Verso.

Barth, Fredrick. 1969. *Ethnic Groups and Boundaries: The Social Organization and Culture Difference*. Long Grove, IL: Waveland Press.

Berkes, Fikret. 1989. "Introduction." Pp. 1–17 in *Common Property Resources: Ecology and Community-Based Sustainable Development*, edited by Fikret Berkes. London: Belhaven Press.

Berkes, Fikret and Carl Folke, eds. 1998. *Linking Social and Ecological Systems: Management Practices and Social Mechanisms for Building Resilience*. Cambridge: Cambridge University Press.

Bian, Yanjie. 2002a. "Institutional Holes and Job Mobility Processes: *Guanxi* Mechanisms in China's Emergent Labor Markets." Pp. 117–136 in *Social Connections in China: Institutions, Culture, and the Changing Nature of Guanxi*, edited by Thomas Gold, Doug Guthrie, and David Wank. Cambridge: Cambridge University Press.

——— 2002b. "Social Capital of the Firm and Its Impact on Performance: A Social Network Analysis." Pp. 275–297 in *Management of Enterprises in People's Republic of China*, edited by Anne S. Tsui and Chung-Ming Lau. Boston, MA: Kluwer Academic Publishers.

Bian, Yanjie and John R. Logan. 1996. "Market Transition and the Persistence of Power: The Changing Stratification in Urban China." *American Sociological Review* 61(5): 739–758.

Boisot, Max and John Child. 1996. "From Fiefs to Clans and Network Capitalism: Explaining China's Emerging Economic Order." *Administrative Science Quarterly* 41(4): 600–628.

Brandt, Loren and Hongbin Li. 2003. "Banking Discrimination in Transition Economies: Ideology, Information, or Incentives?" *Journal of Comparative Economics* 31: 387–413.

Bruun, Ole. 1993. *Business and Bureaucracy in a Chinese City: An Ethnography of Private Business Households in Contemporary China*. Berkeley: Center for Chinese Studies, Institute of East Asian Studies, University of California Press.

1995. "Political Hierarchy and Private Entrepreneurship in a Chinese Neighborhood." Pp. 184–212 in *The Waning of the Communist State: Economic Origins of Political Decline in China and Hungary*, edited by Andrew G. Walder. Berkeley: University of California Press.

Cao, Jinqing. 2009. "Jianchi Tudi Jiating Chengbaozhi Haishi Tudi Siyouhua" (Adhering to the Household Land Contract System or Privatizing Land). *Huazhong Keji Daxue Xuebao (Journal of Huazhong University of Science and Technology)* 23(1): 12–13.

Cao, Yang and Victor Nee. 2000. "Comment: Controversies and Evidence in the Market Transition Debate." *American Journal of Sociology* 105(4): 1175–1189.

Chang, Gordon G. 2001. *The Coming Collapse of China*. New York: Random House.

Chen, Guidi and Chun Tao. 2004. *Zhongguo Nongmin Diaocha (A Survey of Chinese Peasants)*.Beijing: People's Literature Publishing House (Renmin Wenxue Chubanshe).

China Daily. 2004. "China Liberalizes Grain Trading, Pricing," June 4. Retrieved May 10, 2005 (http://www.chinadaily.com.cn/english/doc/2004-06/04/content_336712.htm).

Cui, Zhiyuan. 1993. "China's Rural Industrialization: Flexible Specialization, Moebius-Strip Ownership and Proudhonian Socialism." Unpublished University of Chicago Research Paper. (http://www.cui-zy.cn/Recommended/Personalpapers/CuiRURALIndu.doc)

2000. "How Did Nanjie Village Overcome the Free-Rider Problem?" Translated by Xinyi Wang. *Perspectives* 2 (1). (http://www.oycf.org/Perspectives2/7_083100/how_did_nanjie_village_overcome_.htm) The Chinese version of this article was published in *From Planned Economy to Market Economy*, 1998, Economics, Finance and Trade Publishing Agency of China.

2005. "Liberal Socialism and the Future of China: A Petty Bourgeoisie Manifesto." Pp. 157–174 in *The Chinese Model of Modern Development*, edited by Tian Yu Cao. London and New York: Routledge.

Crowell, Todd and Anne Naham. 1999. "A Communist Theme Park." *Asiaweek* (January 22): 34–37.

Dang, Guoying. 2007. "Jiefang Nongmin de 'Gushi' Haimeiyou 'Jiang'wan" (The "Story" of Peasant Emancipation Has Not Yet Ended). http://zt.cjn.cn/2007zy1hwj/2007zygdpl/200702/t307884.htm.

Deng, Xiaoping. 1994 [1992]. "Excerpts from Talks Given in Wuchang, Shenzhen, Zhuhai and Shanghai." Pp. 361–362 in *Selected Works of Deng Xiaoping: Volume III: 1982–1992*. Beijing: Foreign Languages Press.

Dickson, Bruce J. 2003. *Red Capitalists in China: The Party, Private Entrepreneurs, and Prospects for Political Change*. Cambridge: Cambridge University Press.

DiMaggio, Paul J. and Walter W. Powell. 1983. "The Iron Cage Revisited: Institutional Isomorphism and Collective Rationality in Organizational Field." *American Sociological Review* 48(2): 147–160.

Dore, Ronald. 1983. "Goodwill and the Spirit of Market Capitalism." *British Journal of Sociology* 34(4): 459–482.

Durkheim, Emile. 1973. "Individualism and the Intellectuals." Pp. 43–57 in *Emile Durkheim on Morality and Society*, edited by Robert N. Bellah. Chicago: The University of Chicago Press.

Eckholm, Erik. 1999. "Detour on Capitalist Road: Diehard Maoist Collective." *The New York Times* (January 7), A1, A12.

Edin, Maria. 2003. "State Capacity and Local Agent Control in China: CCP Cadre Management from a Township Perspective." *The China Quarterly* 173: 35–52.

Evans, Peter B. 1989. "Predatory, Developmental and Other Apparatus: A Comparative Political Economy Perspective on the Third World State." *Sociological Forum* 4(4): 561–587.

Evans, Peter B., Dietrich Rueschemeyer, and Theda Skocpol. 1985. *Bringing the State Back In*. Cambridge: Cambridge University Press.

Fei, Xiaotong. 1986. *Xiangtu Zhongguo (Earthbound China)*. Hong Kong: Joint Publishing Co.

Feng, Zhi. 1995. *Wu Renbao Pingzhuan (A Critical Biography of Wu Renbao)*. Beijing: People's Press.

Fukuyama, Francis. 1992. *The End of History and the Last Man*. New York: Free Press.

Gibbs, C.J.N. and D.W. Bromley. 1989. "Institutional Arrangements for Management of Rural Resources: Common Property Regimes." Pp. 22–32 in *Common Property Resources: Ecology and Community-Based Sustainable Development*, edited by Fikret Berkes. London: Belhaven Press.

Gold, Thomas B. 1986. *State and Society in the Taiwan Miracle*. Armonk, NY: M. E. Sharpe.

Gordon, H.S. 1954. "The Economic Theory of a Common-Property Resource: The Fishery." *The Journal of Political Economy* 62(2): 124–142.

Granovetter, Mark. 1985. "Economic Action and Social Structure: The Problem of Embeddedness." *American Journal of Sociology* 91: 481–510.

2005. "The Impact of Social Structure on Economic Outcomes." *Journal of Economic Perspectives* 19(1): 33–50.

Gunn, Christopher. 2000. "Markets against Economic Democracy." *Review of Radical Political Economics* 32: 448–460.

Guthrie, Doug. 2002. "Information Asymmetries and the Problem of Perception: The Significance of Structural Position in Assessing the Importance of *Guanxi* in China." Pp. 37–56 in *Social Connections in China: Institutions, Culture, and the Changing Nature of Guanxi*, edited by Thomas Gold, Doug Guthrie, and David Wank. Cambridge: Cambridge University Press.

Hamilton, Gary G. and Kao Cheng-shu. 1990. "The Institutional Foundations of Chinese Business: The Family Firm in Taiwan." *Comparative Social Research* 12: 95–112.

Hanser, Amy. 2002. "Youth Job Searches in Urban China: The Use of Social Connections in a Changing Labor Market." Pp. 137–162 in *Social Connections in China: Institutions, Culture, and the Changing Nature of Guanxi*, edited by Thomas Gold, Doug Guthrie, and David Wank. Cambridge: Cambridge University Press.

Hardin, Garrett. 1968. "The Tragedy of the Commons." *Science*, New Series 162: 1243–1248.

He, Xuefeng. 2010. *Diquan de Luoji: Zhongguo Nongcun Tudi Zhidu Xiang Hechu Qu (The Logic of Land Rights: Where is China's Rural Land Institution Heading)*. Beijing: China University of Political Science and Law Press.

He, Zhongzhou. 2006. "Nanjie Cun: Sheng yu Shuai (Nanjie Village: Boom and Doom)." *China Newsweek* 271 (April 10): 24–29.

Huang, Yasheng. 2008. *Capitalism with Chinese Characteristics: Entrepreneurship and the State*. New York and London: Cambridge University Press.

Huang, Zongzhi (Philip C. C. Huang). 2010. *Zhongguo de Yinxing Nongye Geming (China's Hidden Agricultural Revolution)*. Beijing: Falü Chubanshe (Law Press).

Huang, Zongzhi and Peng Yusheng. 2007. "San Da Lishixing Bianqian de Jiaohui yu Zhongguo Xiaoguimo Nongye de Qianjing" (The Conjuncture of Three Historic Tendencies and the Prospects for Small-Scale Chinese Agriculture). *Zhongguo Shehui Kexue (Social Sciences in China)* 4: 74–88.

Jacobs, Andrew. 2011. "Village Revolts over Inequalities of Chinese Life." *The New York Times* (December 14).

Jiang, Zemin. 1997. "Hold High the Great Banner of Deng Xiaoping Theory for an All-round Advancement of the Cause of Building Socialism with Chinese Characteristics to the 21st Century." Speech at the 15th National Party Congress of the CCP. (http://www.fas.org/news/china/1997/970912-prc.htm).

2002. "Building an Well-off Society in an All-Round Way and Creating a New Situation in Building Socialism with Chinese Characteristics." Speech at the 16th National Party Congress of the CCP. (http://english.peopledaily.com.cn/200211/18/eng20021118_106983.shtml).

Kornai, Janos. 1992. *The Socialist System: The Political Economy of Communism*. Princeton, NJ: Princeton University Press.

Kwok, Donny. 2010. "Luxury Brands Wrest back China Market, Eye Smaller Cities." Reuters. Retrieved August 20, 2010 (http://www.reuters.com/article/idUSTOE67107820100806).

Li, Cheng. 1997. "Is a Rich Man Happier Than a Free Man? Huaxi Village, China's 'Mini-Singapore.'" Pp. 243–262 in *Rediscovering China: Dynamics and Dilemmas of Reform* by Cheng Li. Lanham, MD: Rowman & Littlefield.

Li, Jingjie. 1994. "The Characteristics of Chinese and Russian Economic Reform." *Journal of Comparative Economics* 18: 309–313.

Li, Lianjiang. 2004. "Political Trust in Rural China." *Modern China* 30(2): 228–258.

Li, Liugen (ed.). 1996. *Linying Xianzhi (History of Linying County)*. Zhengzhou, Henan: Zhongzhou Classical Literature Press.

Li, Ming. 2003. "Legal Move Made to Shield Private Assets." *China Daily Hong Kong Edition*, March 6. Retrieved April 25, 2003 (http://www1.chinadaily.com.cn/hk/2003-03-06/107023.html).

Lin, Nan. 1995. "Local Market Socialism: Local Corporation in Action in Rural China." *Theory and Society* 24: 301–354.

Lin, Nan and Chin-Jou Jay Chen. 1999. "Local Elites as Officials and Owners: Shareholding and Property Rights in Daqiuchuang." Pp. 145–170 in *Property Rights and Economic Reform in China*, edited by Jean C. Oi and Andrew G. Walder. Stanford, CA: Stanford University Press.

Liu, Qian. 2004. *Nanjie Shehui (Nanjie Society)*. Shanghai: Xuelin Press.

Lu, Yuhua. 2004. "Nanjiecun Zhentong (Difficulties Facing Nanjie)." *Shangjie Mingjia (Business Elite)*, March.

Markus, Francis. 2002. "Chinese Village Still in Mao Era." *BBC News World Edition*, November 19. Retrieved May 1, 2006 (http://news.bbc.co.uk/2/hi/asia-pacific/2488905.stm).

Marx, Karl. 1977 [1856]. "Speech at the Anniversary of the *People's Paper*." Pp. 338–339 in *Karl Marx: Selected Writings*, edited by David McLellan. Oxford: Oxford University Press.

Mills, C. W. 1959. *The Sociological Imagination*. Oxford: Oxford University Press.

Montinola, Gabriella, Yingyi Qian, and Barry R. Weingast. 1995. "Federalism, Chinese Style: The Political Basis for Economic Success in China." *World Politics* 48(1): 50–81.

Naughton, Barry. 1994. "What Is Distinctive about China's Economic Transition?: State Enterprise Reform and Overall System Transformation." *Journal of Comparative Economics* 18: 470–490.

Nee, Victor. 1989. "Theory of Market Transition: From Redistribution to Market in State Socialism." *American Sociological Review* 54: 663–681.

1991. "Social Inequalities in Reforming State Socialism: Between Redistribution and Markets in China." *American Sociological Review* 56: 267–282.

1992. "Organizational Dynamics of Market Transition: Hybrid Forms, Property Rights, and Mixed Economy in China." *Administrative Science Quarterly* 37: 1–27.

1996. "Market Transformation and Societal Transformation in Reforming State Socialism." *Annual Review of Sociology* 22: 401–435.

2005. "Organizational Dynamics of Institutional Change: Politicized Capitalism in China." Pp. 53–74 in *The Economic Sociology of Capitalism*, edited by Victor Nee and Richard Swedberg. Princeton, NJ: Princeton University Press.

Nee, Victor and Yang Cao. 1999. "Path Dependent Societal Transformation: Stratification in Hybrid Economies." *Theory and Society* 28: 799–834.

North, Douglass. 1981. *Structure and Change in Economic History*. New York and London: W. W. Norton & Company.

Offer, Avner. 1997. "Between the Gift and the Market: The Economy of Regard." *Economic History Review* 50(3): 450–476.

Oi, Jean. 1999. *Rural China Takes Off: Institutional Foundations of Economic Reform*. Berkeley and Los Angeles: University of California Press.

Oi, Jean and Andrew G. Walder (eds.). 1999. *Property Rights and Economic Reform in China*. Stanford, CA: Stanford University Press.

Ostrom, Elinor. 1990. *Governing the Commons: The Evolution of Institutions for Collective Action*. Cambridge: Cambridge University Press.

Pang, Ruiyin. 2006. *Huaxi Jishi, 2006: Huiwang Wu Renbao (The Stories of Huaxi, 2006: In Retrospect of Wu Renbao)*. Jiangsu: Jiangsu Wenyi Chubanshe.

Parish, William L. and Ethan Michelson. 1996. "Politics and Markets: Dual Transformations." *American Journal of Sociology* 101:1042–1059.

Parris, Kristen. 1993. "Local Initiative and National Reform: The Wenzhou Model of Development." *The China Quarterly* 134: 242–263.

Pearson, Margaret M. 1997. *China's Business Elite: The Political Consequences of Economic Reform*. Berkeley: University of California Press.

Pei, Minxin. 2009. "The Color of China." *The National Interest* (March/April): 13–19.

Peng, Mike W. and Yadong Luo. 2000. "Managerial Ties and Firm Performance in a Transition Economy: The Nature of a Micro-Macro Link." *Academy of Management Journal* 43(3): 486–505.

Polanyi, Karl. 1957 (1944). *The Great Transformation: The Political and Economic Origins of Our Time*. Boston, MA: Beacon Press.

Portes, Alejandro and Julia Sensenbrenner. 1993. "Embeddedness and Immigration: Notes on the Social Determinants of Economic Action." *American Journal of Sociology* 98(6): 1320–1350.

Potter, Pitman B. 2002. "Guanxi and the PRC Legal System: From Contradiction to Complementarity." Pp. 179–196 in *Social Connections in China: Institutions, Culture, and the Changing Nature of Guanxi*, edited by Thomas Gold, Doug Guthrie, and David Wank. Cambridge: Cambridge University Press.

Qi, Jianmin. 2011. "The Debate over 'Universal Values' in China." *Journal of Contemporary China* 20(72): 881–890.

Ramo, Joshua Cooper. 2004. *The Beijing Consensus*. London: Foreign Policy Center.

Rawski, Thomas G. 1994. "Progress without Privatization: The Reform of China's State Industries." Pp. 27–52 in *The Political Economy of Privatization and Public Enterprise in Post-communist and Reforming-Communist States*, edited by Vedat Milor. Boulder, CO: Lynne Rienner Publishers.

Rona-Tas, A. 1994. "The First Shall Be Last? Entrepreneurship and Communist Cadres in the Transition from Socialism." *American Journal of Sociology* 100(1): 40–69.

Rueschemeyer, Dietrich and Peter B. Evans. 1985. "The State and Economic Transformation: Toward an Analysis of the Conditions Underlying Effective Intervention." Pp. 44–77 in *Bringing the State Back In*, edited by Peter B. Evans, Dietrich Rueschemeyer, and Theda Skocpol. Cambridge: Cambridge University Press.

Sachs, Jeffrey D. and Wing Thye Woo. 1994. "Experiences in the Transition to a Market Economy." *Journal of Comparative Economics* 18: 271–275.

Scott, W. Richard. 2001. *Institutions and Organizations*. 2nd edition. Thousand Oaks, CA: Sage Publications.

Shangguan, Jiaoming. 2008. "The Truth of the Development of the 'Red Hundred Million Yuan Village' Nanjie" ('Hongse Yiyuancun' Henan Nanjiecun de Fazhan Zhenxiang). *Nanfang Dushi Bao (Southern Metropolis Daily)*, Feb. 26.

Sherwood, Harriet. 2010. "The Kibbutz: 100 Years Old and Facing an Uncertain Future," *The Guardian*, August 13.

Sicular, Terry. 1996. "Redefining State, Plan and Market: China's Reforms in Agricultural Commerce." Pp. 58–84 in *China's Transitional Economy*, edited by Andrew G. Walder. Oxford: Oxford University Press.

Solinger, Dorothy. 1999. *Contesting Citizenship in Urban China: Peasant Migrants, the State, and the Logic of the Market*. Berkeley and Los Angeles: University of California Press.

Song, Shayin and Fan Yinhuai. 1964. "Dazhai Zhilu (The Path of Dazhai Village)." *People's Daily*, February 10, A1.

Spaeth, Anthony. 1996. "Back to the Future." *Time* (February 5): 27.

Stiglitz, Joseph. 2002. *Globalization and Its Discontents*. New York: W. W. Norton & Company.

Streeck, Wolfgang. 2011. "E Pluribus Unum? Varieties and Commonalities of Capitalism." Pp. 419–455 in *The Sociology of Economic Life*, 3rd edition, edited by Mark Granovetter and Richard Swedberg. Boulder, CO: Westview Press.

Swedberg, Richard. 2005. "The Economic Sociology of Capitalism: An Introduction and Agenda." Pp. 3–40 in *The Economic Sociology of Capitalism*, edited by Victor Nee and Richard Swedberg. Princeton, NJ: Princeton University Press.

Taylor, Frederick Winslow. 1911. *Scientific Management*. New York: Harper and Row.

Wade, Robert. 1988. *Village Republics: Economic Conditions for Collective Action in South India*. Cambridge: Cambridge University Press.

Walder, Andrew G. 1995. "Career Mobility and the Communist Political Order." *American Sociological Review* 60(3): 309–328.

(ed.). 1996. *China's Transitional Economy*. Oxford and New York: Oxford University Press.

2002. "Markets and Income Inequality in Rural China: Political Advantage in an Expanding Economy." *American Sociological Review* 67(2): 231–253.

2003. "Elite Opportunity in Transitional Economies." *American Sociological Review* 68(6): 899–916.

2011. "Transition from State Socialism: A Property Rights Perspective." Pp. 503–525 in *The Sociology of Economic Life*, 3rd edition, edited by Mark Granovetter and Richard Swedberg. Boulder, CO: Westview Press.

Walder, Andrew G. and Jean C. Oi. 1999. "Property Rights in the Chinese Economy: Contours of the Process of China." Pp. 1–24 in *Property Rights and Economic Reform in China*, edited by Jean Oi and Andrew Walder. Stanford, CA: Stanford University Press.

Wan, Jingliang. 2001. "Huaxicun Fangwenji (A Visit to Huaxi Village)." *Shanghai Nongcun Jingji (Shanghai Rural Economy)* 12: 39–44.

Wank, David L. 1995. "Bureaucratic Patronage and Private Business: Changing Networks of Power in Urban China." Pp. 153–183 in *The Waning of the Communist State: Economic Origins of Political Decline in China and Hungary*, edited by Andrew G. Walder. Berkeley: University of California Press.

1996. "The Institutional Process of Market Clientelism: Guanxi and Private Business in a South China City." *China Quarterly* 29: 820–838.

1999. *Commodifying Communism: Business, Trust and Politics in a Chinese City*. Cambridge: Cambridge University Press.

Wang, Shouguo, Li Weihua, Wang Lufeng and Liu Guangchao. 2008. "Investigating Nanjie's Change of Ownership: 'The Economy is Slowly Reviving' after a Difficult Self-Rescue" (Nanjie zhi Bian Diaocha: Jiannan Zijiu hou 'Jingji zheng Fusu'). *Dahe Bao (Dahe Daily)*, March 17.

Weber, Max. 2002 (1904–1905). *The Protestant Ethic and the Spirit of Capitalism: and Other Writings*, translated by Peter Baehr and Gordon C. Wells. New York: Penguin Books.

1951 (1915). *The Religion of China: Confucianism and Taoism*, translated by H.H. Gerth. New York: The Free Press.

1947. *The Theory of Social and Economic Organization*, translated by A.M. Henderson and Talcott Parsons. New York: The Free Press.

Wen, Tiejun. 2008. "Xin Nongcun Jianshe de Zhongdian yu Tudi Siyouhua de Luoji: Huajie Sannong Wenti de Daolu zhi Bian" (The Key Issues of Constructing the New Socialist Countryside and the Logic of Land Privatization: Discerning the Route to Mitigate Rural Problems). *Lü Ye (Green Leaves)* 11: 66–72.

White, Gordon. 1988. *Developmental States in East Asia*. London: Macmillan.

Whiting, Susan. 2001. *Power and Wealth in Rural China: The Political Economy of Institutional Change*. Cambridge: Cambridge University Press.

Whyte, Martin K. 1995. "The Social Roots of China's Economic Development." *The China Quarterly* 144: 999–1019.

1996. "The Chinese Family and Economic Development: Obstacle or Engine?" *Economic Development and Cultural Change* 45: 1–30.

Wong, Christine P.W. 1986. "The Economics of Shortage and Problems of Reform in Chinese Industry." *Journal of Comparative Economics* 10: 363–387.

Woo-Cumings, Meredith. 1999. *The Developmental State*. Ithaca, NY: Cornell University Press.

Woo, Wing Thye. 1994. "The Art of Reforming Centrally Planned Economies: Comparing China, Poland, and Russia." *Journal of Comparative Economics* 18: 276–308.

Wu, Jinglian. 2002. "Nongcun Shengyu Laodongli Zhuanyi yu 'Sannong' Wenti" (The Transfer of Rural Surplus Labor and Rural Issues). *Hongguan Jingji Yanjiu (Macroeconomics)* 6: 6–9.

Wu, Renbao. 2004. "Shijian 'Sange Daibiao' Sixiang Jianshe Fuyu Wenming Xin Huaxi (Practice the Thought of "Three Representatives," Build a New Wealthy and Civilized Huaxi)." Pp. 1–25 in *Huaxi Zhi Lu (The Path of Huaxi)*, Huaxi's promotional material.

Xiaoshuo Hou. 2011. "From Mao to the Market: Community Capitalism in Rural China." *Theory, Culture & Society* 28(2): 46–68.

Xiaoshuo Hou and John Stone. 2008. "The Ethnic Dilemma in China's Industrial Revolution." *Ethnic and Racial Studies* 31(4): 812–817.

Yang, Xiaokai. 2001. "Zhongguo Tudi Suoyouquan Siyouhua de Yiyi" (The Significance of Privatizing Land Ownership in China). Published on April 12 at http://www.aisixiang.com/data/425.html.

Yao, Yang. 2011. *Zhongguo Daolu de Shijie Yiyi (The Global Significance of the Chinese Path)*. Beijing: Peking University Press.

Ye, Xian. 2008. "Xiaogangcun 'Dabaogan' 30 Nian" (30 Years of the Contract System in Xiaogang Village). *Zhongguo Baodao (China Report)* 2: 63–66.

Zang, Xiaowei. 2007. *Ethnicity and Urban Life in China: A Comparative Study of Hui Muslims and Han Chinese*. New York: Routledge.

Zhang, Qian Forrest and John A. Donaldson. 2008. "The Rise of Agrarian Capitalism with Chinese Characteristics: Agricultural Modernization, Agribusiness and Collective Land Rights." *The China Journal* 60: 25–47.

Zhen, Ying. 2003. "Cunzhang Tiqian Yintui Neimu" (Story behind Village Head's Early Retirement). *Beijing Youth Daily (Beijing Qingnian Bao)*, July 17, reproduced at http://www.people.com.cn/BIG5/jingji/1045/1972008.html.

Zhou, Xueguang. 2000. "Economic Transformation and Income Inequality in Urban China: Evidence from Panel Data." *American Journal of Sociology* 105(4): 1135–1174.

2008. "Jiceng Zhengfu jian de 'Gongmou Xianxiang' – Yige Zhengfu Xingwei de Zhidu Luoji" (The Institutional Logic of Collusion among Local Governments in China). *Shehuixue Yanjiu (Sociological Studies)*, 6: 1–21.

# Index

*Adam Smith in Beijing* (Arrighi), 5–6
administration in Chinese government, 8
agribusinesses, 132
agricultural commerce, 4
agricultural cooperatives, 27
agricultural reform, 4–5
agricultural tax, 15
"All Roads Lead to Washington?: Controversies over the China Model", 6
anti rural bias in developmental policies, 15–16
apartments
  in Nanjie, 39–40
  in Shangyuan, 109
appointments of leaders, Nanjie, 67–68
Arrighi, Giovanni, 5–6
associations, Wenzhou, 117
average annual income of Huaxi, 19

banking, 4
  in Huaxi, 87–89
  loans for private enterprises, 11–12
  in Wenzhou, 106, 119–120
Barth, Fredrick, 93–94
*Beijing Consensus* (Ramo), 5–6
Beijing Jingsong Pastry Factory, 38
Bian, Yanjie, 11
Boisot, Max, 11
boldness in Wenzhou culture, 104–105
bonuses for workers, Huaxi, 87–88, 92
boundaries between groups, 93–94, 129
brand image, Wenzhou, 105–106
Brandt, Loren, 11–12
brickworks, Nanjie, 36–37
Buddhism, 112–113

bureaucracy-market interaction, 8
business practices, Nanjie, 57

cadre elite, 7
cadres, 8, 10, 100–101
  in Huaxi, 82
  land disputes, 17
  promotion system, 17
  in Shangyuan, 113–114
capable persons, 34
capitalistic values among Chinese, 2
Central Plain Flour Mill, 35, 36–39
Chambers of Commerce, Wenzhou, 117
Chen, Shuxin, 68
Child, John, 11
China model (*zhongguo moshi*), 5–6, 9
*China Statistical Yearbook 2009* (*zhongguo tongji nianjian 2009*), 16
Chinese Communist Party (CCP), 2, 3–4, 26, 121
Chint, 117, 119
Christianity, 112–113
"circle on the outside, square on the inside" slogan, 19, 57–63
Civil Code, 102
clientelist ties between local state officials and private entrepreneurs, 8, 10
cluster economy, Wenzhou, 106, 127
codes of conduct
  Nanjie, 58–59, 125
  overview, 58
collective economy, villagers opinions of, 118
collective enterprises, Nanjie, 68–69
collective living allowance, Shangyuan, 109
collective ownership of land, 122–124

Huaxi Cultural and Ethical Development
  Company, 94–95
Huaxi Forging Factory, 78
Huaxi Grain and Fodder Processing Factory,
  The, 75
Huaxi Group Corporation, 78
Huaxi Model, 94–95, 96
Huaxi Village, 71–96
  culture and ideology, 94–96
  history of, 72–80
  institutional structures, 125, 126–127
  overview, 19
  patriarchal system of management, 80–86
  pattern of economic flow, 123–124
  social networks, 128
  system of distribution, 87–94
Hui Muslims, 28
*hukou* system, 18, 26
  Huaxi, 89
  Shangyuan, 116
human capital, 130–131
Hungary, 5

ideology
  in Huaxi, 94–96
  Mao Zedong Thought, 51, 59, 64–66
illegal fundraising, Huaxi, 92
incentive structure
  for government agencies and officials, 133
  in Huaxi, 126
  in Nanjie, 67, 125–126
  for villages, 127
income
  average annual, Huaxi, 19
  of cadres, Shangyuan, 113–114
  in Huaxi, 77, 91–94
  in Nanjie, 45–47, 49–50, 56–57
individual enterprises, 99–100
industrial output
  of Huaxi, 19
  of Shangyuan, 110
Industrial Trading Company, 111
industrialization, Nanjie, 31–39
instant noodles production, Nanjie, 37–39,
  57–58
institutional change in post-socialist societies,
  6–7
institutional isomorphism, 97
institutional structures, 124–127
Internet access, Nanjie, 51
internship labor market, Huaxi, 93
interpretive case method, 135

intra-party democracy initiatives, 4
Israeli kibbutzim, 14, 126

Japan
  social networks in market, 10
  Yamagishi villages, 14
Jiang, Zemin, 101–102
Jingbang Village, 79
Juling Agricultural Cooperative, 27

kibbutzim, 14, 126
kinship
  in Huaxi leadership, 83–86
  importance in development of private
    economy, 9
  in Shangyuan, 112
  in Wenzhou businesses, 106, 119–120

labor unions, 18
land systems
  agricultural production in Nanjie, 29–31
  in China, 122–124
  disputes over, 17
  household responsibility system, 4
  in Huaxi, 76
  in Nanjie, 58, 59
  privatization, 20–21
  in Shangyuan, 108–109, 110–111
  in Wenzhou, 107–108
laws favoring private enterprises, 101–102
leaving villages, cost of
  in Huaxi, 88–89
  in Nanjie, 58
Li, Hongbin, 11–12
liberal democracy, 3–4
Lin, Nan, 7
Linying County Utility Bureau, 39
liquor customs in Henan's culture, 61
littoral pattern, 33
Liushi Electrical Equipment General Factory,
  110–111
loans for private enterprises, 11–12
local competition, Shangyuan, 119–120
local governments
  corruption in, 17
  Huaxi, 125, 126–127
  incentive structure, 133
  Nanjie, 125–126
  patterns describing role in economic
    activities, 31–33
  peasant burdens, 15
  political-institutional structure, 16–17

Printed in the United States
By Bookmasters